J. IGNACIO TELLECHEA IDÍGORAS

THE STRANGE BIRD
BROTHER ZACARÍAS

SAN SEBASTIAN 2000

DL : SS-156/2000

ISBN: 84-607-0153-0

Michelena artes gráficas, s.l. - Astigarraga (Gipuzkoa)

To José María Ucín,
who made me write this book

"In his freely-given donation to man, God is subject to no law. And it has nothing to do with sociologists or psychologists; at best, the object is the relationship, religious, so to speak, between man and that which is known as the Absolute. Even I, this unique being, to whom the only God gives himself, am subject to no general law. Thus, in my relationship with God, one that must adapt to God's relationship with me, I am alone; no one else can understand it, no one else can explain it or intermediate in it. As every man dies alone, so every man prays alone, every man must enter the *chamber* before his Father from Heaven, and understand and do the Will that God has for him, only for him. And nobody else can enter that chamber for him"

Hans Urs von Balthasar

THE STRANGE BIRD

The bird! Everyone remembers the bird. It is true that a bird flying into a great church is hardly an everyday occurrence, particularly when it flies under its ogives. And even stranger is that with the church crammed with people it should dive down from the heights in mid-mass and settle on a coffin in the centre of the temple, in front of an altar surrounded by a throng of people. Naturally, all eyes turned to the bird, momentarily forgetting the service. The officiating priest, Abbot Mariano, had already started to say the Our Father. And just then something even stranger and more unexpected occurred: the bird suddenly took to the air again and jumped from the coffin onto the shoulder of the officiating Abbot.

Patently surprised at the unexpected visit, he hesitated for a few seconds, not really knowing what to do, and then took the bird, which surprisingly offered no resistance, kissed its little head and passed it on to the nearest concelebrant, although he broke the silence with a mysterious phrase: "I think that this bird is Brother Zacarías, always bound to his Abbot, obeying him in all his deeds and work, and who never did anything without my consent. I think he has come to ask for my permission… even to go to Heaven".

Brother Zacarías had died the previous day, on the feast of Saint Bernard. The brethren found him dead at five o'clock in the morning, after Matins. He was getting ready to celebrate the feast of his great Saint, Saint Bernard. The Archbishop of Pamplona, Monsignor Cirarda, came to say the mass. How do you combine feast and mourning?

“When a monk dies”, the current Abbot, Francisco, tells me, “Believe you me, we feel great pain, as it is a brother who has left us after many years together. But at the same time, we feel great inner peace, because our brother has reached his destination, he is with God! At the solemn mass that morning, with Zacarías’ corpse resting in a side chapel, the Archbishop sowed the seeds of optimism, beginning his sermon with these words: “Today we celebrate the feasts of two saints, Saint Bernard and Saint Zacarías…”

As usual, the monastery of La Oliva published no obituary. The news of his death spread by word of mouth. The next morning, August 21, 1986, the bells of La Oliva, the beautiful Cistercian temple sited near Carcastillo were ringing out, and its church was crammed with people who had come from all around to say the last goodbye to the good Brother. And the expression *the last goodbye* comes from force of habit, because those who knew him and had had contact with him were sure that those words so often sung at funerals “because the life of those who believe in you, My Lord, does not end, it is transformed…” would be true of Zacarías.

Some years have gone by. I am sure that no one remembers the sermon given by Father Mariano, the Abbot of the monastery, but I am equally sure that everyone who attended the funeral that morning remembers the bird, that strange bird.

By the way, the person who actually received the little bird from the hands of the Abbot was at a loss as to what to do with the poor little creature. The rubrics, those meticulous rules which dictate everything that has to be done in the liturgy, make no provision for what to do if someone thrusts a bird on you mid-mass... the good monk had the brainwave of stuffing the little bird into the pockets of his broad white habit, subsequently proceeding to follow mass devoutly. The bird had suffocated by the end of the service, although it had fulfilled its symbolic duty and delivered its message. I shall tell you that it was discreetly buried next to Zacarías in the small plot of ground where his tomb lies. Thus, symbol and what it symbolised, united, share the holy ground of the silent cemetery of La Oliva.

I never actually had any dealings with brother Zacarías. Neither do I recall if I ever encountered him in the course of my visits to the monastery, when I used to drop in to see an old teacher, one who had taught me in my first year at Seminary, and who was later my co-disciple in Rome, José Sotero Aguirre. However, someone that did know Zacarías, and who felt profound veneration for him, came to see me after his death to ask me to write something about him. From the outset he wanted me to come to the monastery so that I could soak up the atmosphere and also meet some people that had known him.

It was in August. My friend, who had also witnessed the incident with the little bird at the funeral, wanted me to focus on the other bird, not the symbolic one, but the real bird, brother Zacarías. He wanted me to find out who he was, describe him, make him known. He felt deeply bound to him, spiritually "touched" by him. My job was to capture him, or should I say hunt him? –although in any event it was I who was being captured and captivated by the mysterious brother Zacarías.

So one fine day in August I repaired yet again to the monastery of La Oliva, this time with a new objective.

We lunched with the monks in the simple dining room, and they read to us during the meal, as in my seminary days. In the afternoon I was fortunate to be able to address the whole community in the following or similar terms:

> "I have been asked to write a few words about brother Zacarías. I neither knew him nor had any dealings with him. You, on the other hand, did. I imagine that your Brother left no lengthy texts with spiritual revelations or messages, and that nor did he ever reveal his spiritual adventures in any depth. As silence is a basic law among you –and was even more so in not so far-off times– neither, I suppose, did you have the chance to engage in lengthy discussions with your brother. But you did live with him, you know his life here well, and you must have crossed the occasional word with him. These memories will be like beautiful flowers. Could you gift me some of them so that I can make up a humble, but undoubtedly sweet-smelling and beautiful bouquet? You may omit your names, but I would ask those of you who do respond to say how many years you lived alongside him. I will give the Abbot a list of very simple questions. If you help me then I will try to write something about this brother, who I know was loved and venerated by all."

That was how I sowed the seeds of my proposal. Without haste, without anguish. How could anyone conceive haste in that mansion where time seems to have stood still, transcending eternity?

A good few months elapsed without any news for me when I returned to La Oliva the following summer, en route to Zaragoza. The Abbot had a surprise for me: a folder with the answers of many monks, who had been close colleagues of Zacarías. A few hours later I was summoned to Zaragoza: Zacarías' brother, a priest whose ministry was in Venezuela, had just arrived. It was probably a one-and-only chance to get acquainted with a chapter that had died and been buried in the monastery: the past, the pre-monastic life of Zacarías. I was with him in a few hours, and the next day we travelled together to Oteiza la Solana, the town where Zacarías was born and had grown up. I later had the chance to talk to the good women who looked after him in the Hospital in Pamplona in the months leading up to his death.

Zacarías, in the beginning little more than a name to me, began to take shape. Moreover, it was striking how all the people I have met over the years who had known Zacarías invariably responded, on being asked by me about him, with the utmost simplicity, aplomb and laconism: "Zacarías? A saint! A cut above the rest!"

Nothing more... and nothing less. They could hardly be conversant with the severe rules issued by Pope Urban VIII in the 18th Century, strictly forbidding the use of the word saint for anyone who had never been officially canonised by the Church. Abbot Mariano is aware of them, however. That is why I was stunned to hear him say, utterly seriously, and knowing better than anyone that Cistercian monks are rarely chosen as candidates for canonisation or beatification: "One day we shall see Zacarías on the altar." He was Zacarías' Abbot, so what better insight into the innermost depths of Zacarías' soul than his?

In the meantime, something unthinkable has happened to my friend José María. For the first time ever, and in broad daylight, a bird entered his spacious living room. It was not a common sparrow, nor a bright canary. It fluttered round the room several times before settling on a picture frame. He had time to take numerous photos of it. Suddenly, it dawned on him: it was the twentieth of August, the anniversary of Zacarías' death. It was he, he who had come to see his friend and bolster his determination to make him known, to encourage him to finish what he had started. Some days later, intrigued by the visit of that strange bird, he went to see some friends, ornithologists, who identified the animal immediately. It was a Zebra finch (*Poephila Taeniopygia Guttata*), sporting its unmistakeable marks on the throat and striped breast and tail. Don't ask me where it had come from or escaped from. One of the photographs of the birds adorned the cover of the *El Mundo* newspaper that 20th of August.

I am also beginning to think that Zacarías had come to chase me up, to make me finally take pen to paper. So it is time to get down to work. I am sure that many will thank me for it. It is not up to me to canonise Zacarías. I would be happy if I managed to open up his jar of perfume and let everyone partake of the perfume of his "saintly life".

An old Franciscan tertiary, an ecstatic and preacher as well, who died in 1536 –known as Santa Juana in the village of Cubas, where she died– said that people were imbued with refreshed and finely-honed virtues, like "the fresh and sweet-smelling flower when it is born, and therefore do the will of God as the sweet-smelling flower pleases the person who smells it, and a great deal more." And anyone who reads these pages, written with devotion, is hereby invited to simply smell, take a deep breath, of this "fresh and sweet-smelling flower."

I

A FEW HOURS IN OTEIZA

It is true that a saint is not born, but that he is made. But it is no less true that he must be born first, and what is more, somewhere and sometime. The place is permanent, although it may change as the years ago by. But time is utterly mobile, it never stops. In order to give Zacarías a time and a space, let us say that he was born in Oteiza de la Sotana on June the 10th, 1907. In the land of Estella, as they say in Navarra. He was baptised the next day and confirmed on November 15th, 1908.

That land was fertile in vocations: Capuchins, Claretians, charity school monks, all of the Word of God. They are scattered all over the world: Venezuela, Mexico, Colombia. I would like to mention one whom I actually knew. He was born in Oteiza 20 years before Zacarías: Arcadio Larraona, who with the passing of time became a Claretian monk, an eminent canonical professor in Rome, and a Cardinal of the Holy Church, greatly esteemed by Paul the Sixth. He died in 1973 in the Eternal City.

How different were the paths reserved for these two natives of Oteiza! Baptised in the same parish church, both of them grew in piety, gazing at the magnificent altarpiece presided by a graceful St Michael, flanked by St Peter and St Paul. On the side altars stood Saint Joseph and Our Lady of the Rosary. In their childhood they would listen to the "dawn singers", who as the day dawned would break the morning silence with the verses of the Rosary in October. They would also attend the processions of the chapels of El Salvador and Tirso, running about in the village square on the feast of St John, where I too was an onlooker. That selfsame square where the Town Hall was erected in 1982 to replace its 18th-Century predecessor, which had been demolished.

Oteiza stands on a hill commanding a marvellous view, revealing myriad towns and villages: Lerín, Baigorri, Larraga, Artajona, Miranda de Arga, Muniain, Morentin,... and the side of the mythical Montejurra. Many Basque place names still live on in Oteiza: Balsaberria, Otazua, Mendigibel, Litxarra, Zamaka, Legardeta, Ezkibileta... and no fewer surnames: Landa, Arandia, Mendía, Echeberría, Azcona, Goicoetxea. The monument to those who died in the Civil War bears others: Zudaire, Zabala, Irisarri, Inza, Echeberri, Irigoyen, Iguzquiza, Urbiola, Lizasoain, Arizala, etc. Eutimio Aramendía, a hospital monk who was murdered in the war and beatified in 1992, is not among them.

Oteiza is a region of dry land. I used to go to the Idoia pond to water the cattle. The lower pond was made just before 1924 to provide the village with water. Wheat and barley are now grown, vineyards and olive groves once abounded. Threshing floors, grape presses, farmyards, carts and dust made up the village-scape. At that time Oteiza was a major livestock centre for oxen, mules, cattle, donkeys; as well as livestock for eating, mainly swine and poultry. All these animals used to perform their daily concerto or symphony, at dawn or dusk, a sure sign of life, hustle and bustle and hard work.

There was plenty of work to be had for all, all day long in some seasons, so unemployment did not rear its head. In such a setting and climate, strength, hard work and strong character were the order of the day. And this was the school of life where Zacarías grew up, and was later condemned by life to additional other trials and tribulations, and harsh ones at that!

His mother and father did not last long, leaving four orphans from their last marriage and a further four from previous marriages. Zacarías was the eldest of the first batch, and it was he who was most aware of the magnitude of the tragedy. The children were farmed out to different families, some of them even outside the village. However, let us not jump the gun, because this chapter on the family is a very serious and decisive one, as in cases like the one in hand the family tree is not cleanly vertical, but has intricate branches. Nevertheless, paperwork alone would have doomed my investigation to failure, or would at best have rendered it sorely lacking, had Providence, in the form of José Santamaría, or to be more specific Monsignor parish priest of Altragracia in Quibor (Venezuela), not come to my aid. Unshackled by papers, and simply by digging into his memory, he told me a very complicated story. I trust you will be able to follow it.

The paternal grandfather, the second son of the Santamaría family, of the Casa Margota In Villanueva de Yerri, in the lands of Estella, left the family home for Oteiza to marry a widow who already had an heiress, Nicanora Morrás. And thus, the son of this second marriage, Tirso Santamaría Morrás, was already excluded by birth from the inheritance by virtue of common law, and could aspire only to “legitimacy”. Which is why he had to abandon the family home.

First of all he wed a girl from the Iturmendi family in Los Arcos, with whom he had two children, Antonio and Julia Santamaría Iturmendi. Tirso would father Zacarías.

His mother, Veremunda Aramendía Morentín, married a lad from the Inda family, with whom she had two children: Pedro and Domingo Inda Aramendía, and then she too became a widow…

After losing their spouses from their first marriages, Tirso and Veremunda were wed and had four children:

ZACARIAS
Dionisio
Francisca
José

who bore the surnames Santamaría Aramendía Morrás and Moretin. Let us now jump to what was then the future, and now past, destiny of these eight children from three marriages. As custom would had it in homes in Navarra at the time (and until not so long ago as well), five of these children embraced the religious life.

Yes, I knew that it was necessary to get rid of some hungry months from the home, but let us not forget the deeply-rooted religious tradition in those families, who delighted in having a priest or children of some religious standing among them. I will never forget the first Mass in Rome of my dear friend José María Cabodevilla, more than 40 years ago.

It was in the convent of the Servants of Mary, the so-called “Siervicas”. Of a 42-strong community of nuns, 36 of them were from Navarra—in Rome! They sang *jotas* after mass and some of them even danced –after closing the doors– to the melodies of their native land, ably accompanied on the accordion by the priest José María Herrero, who also hailed from Navarra.

So, five of the children of this jumble of marriages, offspring and surnames took to the religious life:

Pedro Inda Iturmendi became a Claretian missionary, and was posted to Argentina while still very young, where he died in 1950.

Julia Santamaría, who studied at the boarding school of the Daughters of Saint Joseph in Pamplona’s Magdalena district, also joined the Congregation later, was also posted to Argentina, where he died at some point in the nineteen fifties.

ZACARÍAS Santamaría Aramendía, born in 1907, joined the monastery of La Oliva in 1929, where he remained until his death on August 20, 1986.

Francisca Santamaría Aramendía, who also went to the boarding school of the Daughters of Saint Joseph, attended the Pamplona school of La Magdalena and died in the Residence of The Congregation in Granollers (Catalonia) in 1987.

Monsignor José Santamaría Aramendía, my magnificent informant, was born in 1915, joined the Claretian Seminary in 1926 and took his Holy Orders in 1929 in Segovia. A missionary in Venezuela, and appointed Cardinal to the dioceses of Barquismento (1967), he worked as a priest in Quibor. John Paul II named him Monsignor on his Golden Anniversary as a Priest (1989).

The information seems very terse and cold, although in the words of Monsignor Santamaría it is transformed into warm, vivid, existential memories. I took good advantage of his trip to Spain to catch an exciting story of his and his family's past from the horse's mouth. I had good reason for doing so. Even now, at the ripe old age of 80, he is a living archive of vivid memories:

> *"In 1940, when I came to my village (Oteiza) to preach the sermon of St. Michael, the Patron Saint of the parish, all the grandmothers of the village congratulated me, but there was one among them who said to me, with deep conviction: "It is now very clear that your father, Tirso, was a good and saintly man! You were orphaned when you were all very young, but look at your family now, so many nuns, and you, a priest. Tirso was such a good man!*
>
> *And that is true, he continues. That is what Tirso was like. A great man, industrious, well-liked and respected. He had been a Sergeant in the War in the Philippines, and later became the constitutional mayor of Oteiza. A staunch Catholic. Even when he took ill he went to mass and took communion daily. Sometimes, when I went to see Zacarías at La Oliva, he would say to me: Come let us say the Rosary as father used to at home. Those were our roots, deep and fresh, auguring a plentiful harvest. Zacarías, the eldest brother, was barely 12 when we lost our mother and father. My mother died giving birth to me.*

On the death of my father, around 1919, Antonio and Julia, born of the first marriage, went to live with their grandparents in Margota In Villanueva de Yerri. I was taken to Mendigorría, to the family of Pedro Alfaro-Fidela Iruzum, who had lost a son my age. That was my father's deathbed wish.

Zacarías, being the eldest, stayed at home, although he did not agree with any of this. One day –he must have been about 15 years old– he turned up in Mendigorría and eventually said to me: you don't belong here. Do you want to come home? Well, just wait for me by the bridge. And thus he deceitfully and bodily dragged me away from my new family, much to their great anguish. Years later, when he was a monk, he asked them to forgive him, they who had been so generous to us. But the simple truth is this that he, the first-born, wanted to keep the family together. When I was still a child, he would sometimes ask me my surname, and if I replied Santamaría Aramendía Alfaro Oteiza, he would promptly thump me and then correct the third and fourth surnames: Morrás Morentin.

We, brothers and sisters, lived as a family. Zacarías and Dionisio worked the fields. I went to school. My poor sister Francisca was but 12 years old and had to cope with all the housework: meals, washing, etc. We were still children and it was almost impossible to run the house properly. But is was in such hardship that Zacarías' two greatest qualities stood out: his responsibility as head of the family, and his harshness in correcting us and punishing the younger brothers and sisters.

He spared the rod with nobody, not even little Francisca. Later, when he became a monk he also begged us to forgive him for having treated us so harshly, and he adored Francisca with gently delicacy. Their respective positions kept them apart for many years, but I know when Zacarías died in 1986 he called Francisca to heaven a year later, to keep her close by him, and safer.

A few years went by and our family broke up after a family council: young Francisca and her older sister went to the boarding school of the Josefinas de Pamplona, where she would later take her vows. They found me a home with Nicanora Aramendía until I joined the Claretian seminary in Santo Domingo de la Calzada in 1926. Our other two brothers and sisters were taken in by the older brother, Domingo Inda: Dionisio stayed there until he married after the Spanish Crusade (1940), whereas Zacarías stayed on until he joined the army.

Separated physically, and by some seven or eight years, my memories of Zacarías at the time are rather vague and imprecise. I remember that he told me, then a monk, how before going to work in the fields he would stuff some of the few remaining holy books that had belonged to our father into his saddle bags. In one of them, probably the Christian Year, *he read the story of a monk who had committed a solitary sin but never dared to confess it, not even on his death bed. Buried under the monastery choir stall, one day his tomb was opened and a voice was heard: Let me out of here! Stunned by that gruesome tale, Zacarías had turned to another man who was working alongside him and asked him about this solitary sin business. Did he have the same problem? Anyway, God gave him illumination and helped him to set his life straight.*

I did not live with him for long, and neither did I have a lot of contact with him. Our father was kind, but

Zacarías was harsh. I saw him as someone special, rather strange and out of place, out of tune with the lifestyle of the life style of the lads of our village at the time. He was rather withdrawn, and frequented the church and prayed. At that time in the village there were Spiritual Exercises for men only in the church up the road. I am sure he attended them, as they were held very near his own house.

Zacarías had a sad, indefinable smile, melancholic and mysterious. I am sure that he felt sort of off-centre, he wanted to break away from something, look for something. What and how? He must have sought advice from someone. In any event, when he turned eighteen, and in order to gain his freedom and leave his small world behind him, he signed up in the army as a volunteer to do what was then obligatory military service anyway. More than once he told me of how he had gone to Pamplona for the sanfermines *(bull fights) in the company of others who proposed going to a brothel and tried to drag him along with them. He escaped from them and lost them. Even then he had a way with words. Sometimes the most difficult part is to break away from ties that bind, recover your freedom, and then things start to run more smoothly. Zacarías wanted to leave the village behind, have the chance to pray and meditate, to be able to face up to what life had in store for him. And he did just that.*

I have been told that Zacarías had a girlfriend, although I think that at his age it could hardly have been serious or definitive. She was one of the girls of the Doncel family, one of the most important families in Villanueva de Yerri. He must have met her at the local fiestas, perhaps Santa Cruz, which he used to spend at Casa Margota, our grandparents' home. Zacarías would have been about 16 or 17 at most, because he was a soldier at that age. She married one of the sons of the good family of Arizala and I know they went to see Zacarías at La Oliva amid great joy and peace of mind. What happened afterwards was very nice, although you already know that anyway, and will be able to tell the story yourself.

What I do know of the Pamplona period is that he was posted to the Constitution Regiment, which later became known as the America Regiment. At that time, in his free time Zacarías would go to the small church of San Fermín de Aldapa. I don't know if he talked to any of the Corazonista Fathers that had preached in Oteiza. What I do know is that the neighbours used to watch the soldier make his afternoon visit to the church and then return to the barracks. They called him the "little soldier of the Constitution."

There was someone else who watched him carefully, the priest Onofre Larumbre, incumbent of the Holy Church Cathedral, and a frequent visitor to that convent and church. A deeply religious man, and a great lover of the Arts and Archaeology, he was determined to recover the old Monastery of La Oliva, near Carcastillo, to subsequently return it to the old Cistercian Order it had belonged to up until the so-called desamortización[T.N.]*. Onofre had just finished relocating a community from the monastery of Getafe, near Madrid, to the Navarran*

[T.N.] The *desamortización* in Spain refers to a series of laws which made it possible to sell off assets or properties belonging to the so called "dead hands" or those who could not sell them, such as the crown, the Church or nobles. A large part of the church's heritage was publicly auctioned throughout the 19th Century in this process.

monastery of La Oliva, and had called upon the County Council and other authorities in Navarra to materially restore the monastery, which was steeped in centuries of history, as he dreamt of restoring its spirituality. But vocations were needed to do so. This is why Onofre struck up a relationship with the strange "little soldier of the Constitution", delving into his soul, into his as yet unformed desires, and became his teacher and mentor. It must have been Onofre who redirected him towards La Oliva.

But before that Zacarías finished his military service in Africa, where he graduated. As the date to join the community approached, Zacarías was brimming with inner and deep-seated joy. He did not even venture to Oteiza to see his family. Such was his haste that he went straight from the barracks to the monastery, without even taking off his uniform, The "little soldier of the Constitution" thus saw his dearest dream come true, and one fine day decided to knock on the door of La Oliva monastery.

A drawing of the Australian chaffinch

This all happened around August 1928. The unpolished and melancholic young man found his way, and embarked upon his adventure. Young people, who so often feel and believe that they are footloose and fancy-free, tend to be little more than poor slaves of their environment and surrounds, which bind them from head to foot, like dolls. Beware of the tyrannical routine of the work gang or squad, so difficult to avoid, then and now! Beware of the irresistible pressure of countless forces that *programme* and destroy the freedom and liberty of young people! The journey from Pamplona to Carcastillo must have seemed eternal to the young man, possessed as he was by indefinable anxiety. Perhaps he completed the stretch from Carcastillo to La Oliva on foot. He reached the door and crossed the threshold. On the other side... the much yearned-for silence and solitude. But God was at the end. He joined the community on August 16th, 1928.

II

BEHIND THE DOOR... A LONG STORY

He who expectantly knocks at the door of a monastery, intending to enter it and stay there, is not unlike one in love: the latter believes that he and he alone has discovered love. The little soldier, determined to join the community of La Oliva, and without even taking off his uniform, must have felt like the first person ever to do so. After a while, however, he would have realised that a whole community dwelt therein, which had therefore pre-empted him, although he was undoubtedly unaware of the centuries of history that lay behind that door. He was there on the advice of Onofre, who was well acquainted with his deepest and darkest desires. He had placed a magical name, hitherto unknown to him, in his mind: "Take the bus to Carcastillo, La Oliva is a few stops before it, you will see a church with a very high façade."

As easy as that.

How could he, whose little schooling had been garnered at the village school of Oteiza, have known that the monastery of Santa María de La Oliva had been founded almost eight hundred years before that? A majestic building completed in 1199, whose domain had gradually spread to the lands of Navarra and Aragón, with the help of popes, the monarchs of Navarra and the faithful. Its Abbott enjoyed feudal rights over many of the neighbouring villages; the black death and the Civil War between the Trastamaras in far-off centuries had razed the population and tributes. The monastery made a timid recovery in the Fifteenth Century; Phillip II attempted to annex it to the so-called Congregation of Castille, making it independent of its French origins; the monastery was turned into a hospital during the war of the Convention (1794-5); it was looted, like so many others, by Napoleon's troops in 1808, its community was dissolved in 1809 and restored by Ferdinand VII in 1814 and exclaustered in 1821, reunited in 1923 and disappeared definitively in the exclaustration and *desamortización* of 1835. After a silent and dark parenthesis of almost one hundred years, new life was breathed into the monastery yet again by his friend Onofre Larumbe, President of the Commission of Monuments, who, in 1930, issued a manifesto in favour of La Oliva, which "lay in ruins... desolate and barren, a nest for vermin and a shelter for livestock."

When Zacarías knocked at its door, the new Community, which had arrived from Val de San José, near Getafe, had been there barely two years. After several years as a Priory, it received its first Abbot in 1945. Zacarías would come to know four abbots:

Father José Olmedo Arrieta (1945-47)

Father Plácido Arena Azcarate (1957-62)

Father Bernardo Ben, Superior (1962-69)

Father Mariano Crespo, Superior (1969-72), and Abbot (1972-03)

Father Francisco Sánchez, current Abbot (1993-__)

But that rather dilapidated mansion, its cloister and chapterhouse, its superb church with three naves and huge apse, the great gothic entrance door and the ruins of other rooms of the monastery all bore eloquent witness to its venerable age, and all was imbued with silence and the far-off murmur of ancient prayer. It was a different world, so removed from the familiar church of Oteiza, or the barracks he had just left behind in Pamplona!

As time went by he too would delve into the mystery of those silent stones, learning that Santa María de La Oliva was a link in a long chain, one of a network of monasteries scattered over Spain, all of them with venerable names: Fitero, the first of them all, not far away, under the protective shadow of Saint Raymond of Burgundy –and where would Burgundy be for Zacarías?– Veruela, Piedra, Rueda, Valdediós, Huerta, Sacramenia, Valbuena, Palazuelos, Valparaíso, Morereula, Valdeiglesias –so many valleys!– Poblet, Santes Creus, Sobrado, Osera, Meira, La Real, Valdigna... all of them in the lands of Aragón, Castille, Asturias, Majorca, Valencia, Galicia... Oh, and in Navarra, Leyre and Irache as well. However, that harvest had come from France. The "white monks" as they were known for some time, to distinguish them from the black ones, the Benedictines, from whom the whites had come.

Once part of the family, he would gradually learn its long and ancient history. Three monks, whom a modern historian called "rebels", had started the adventure: Robert, the Benedictine Abbot of Molesmes, Alberic and

Steven Harding. They were the driving force behind the new adventure. Benedictine monks of the dyed black habit. Their rebelliousness was peculiar, and has been oft repeated throughout history! They belonged to the most important monastic Order in the West, which had spread throughout Europe, studding it with no less venerable names. Its greatest star was justly named Saint Benedict, the Father of the West. They were steeped in centuries of history. Saint Benedict of Nursia physically fled from the Roman society of the decadent Empire, passionately seeking solitude, and attracted many followers: all they wanted to be was Christians, but serious ones: their motto was ORA ET LABORA.

When the old structures of the Europe of the Roman Empire crumbled, spawning the advent of new people that spoke strange tongues and invaded everything, the Benedictine monasteries were small citadels, islands of peace, focal points of spiritual solace, seedbeds of popes, bishops, missionary monks, writers. It was thanks to them that the wealth of ancient Christian and pagan culture was conserved. The most ancient classic Greco-Roman codices, now rare treasures of national libraries, all come from the ancient Benedictine monasteries. Without them the history of Europe would have been utterly different. Cluny and his fabulous spiritual irradiation outside France is a capital chapter of our western culture. Their monasteries were oases of prayer and culture. Their *scriptoria*, or writing workshops, saved innumerable works from disappearing. Their artistic refinement created spaces suited to that life: churches, cloisters, chapter rooms. The techniques they used to work the land, with the help of a staunch family of converts and settlers, contributed to the material evolution of those centuries. Their power and influence spread, as did their weight with popes and kings, their possessions, the grandness and refinement of their mansions, in the midst of that feudal society.

And this is where the aforementioned rebelliousness comes in. The initial monastic action, deeply spiritual, was encumbered by an onerous and extra burden. They had to go back to the origins. The three "rebels" of our story did not aim to found a new order, but simply recover their original *raison d'être* with a stricter loyalty to the Rule of Saint Benedict. Robert of Molesmes withdrew with some twenty followers to a new site, Cistercium, Cîteaux. Their undertaking was driven by austerity, simplicity, greater solitude, all inspired by a total love for and a life in Christ, which was to be followed strictly. Free of vocational secretariats or recruitment campaigns, the action of the three rebels brought unexpected consequences, namely the spontaneous influx of people also seeking to embrace this new existence.

Their monasteries relinquished the artistic refinement of the great Benedictine abbeys. The stark, sober lines of their temples and cloisters dispensed with the marvellous capitals and columns of the Cluny style. The habit was the plain colour of the wool or linen, without being dyed black. Choral chants were sparse, free of the intricate adornments of the Gregorian chant. There were no distractions. Greater solitude and isolation was deliberately sought in the places where monasteries were sited. They reverted to the manual work of the monk in the field, without delegating such tasks to settlers, although this work was rapidly taken over by convert brethren. There was a return to poverty, to austerity, to a harder life.

Just after this new way of life was born it was embraced by Bernard and his brethren, the sons of a noble family. Saint Bernard was the leading light in that movement, and was followed by many others, although he was not a founder of the Cistercian Order, and nor was he Head Abbot of the constellation of renovated monasteries. Yes, it is true that they sought secluded and solitary sites for their monasteries, and felled forests, rototilled the land and brought about an agricultural revolution with their techniques and by selling their surpluses. In recent times, when the Marxist tide prevailed in our Universities, there was one lecturer who referred his pupils to the exclusive research of rototilled land, as if Saint Bernard had been nothing but an agricultural engineer or a forerunner of the FAO. I actually had to ask some of these students, absorbed in that gruelling research to the point of obsession: Do you have the remotest notion of who Saint Bernard was, an arbiter of 12th-Century Europe, revered by Popes and Monarchs alike, engaged in a heated debate with Abelardo, a prolific and sweet writer, one of Luther's favourites, etc.? Do you know that the whole of Europe has prayed to the Virgin Mary for centuries throught Saint Bernard's "Remember"? Of course the poor and impoverished students were absolutely ignorant of all this. Talk about getting the wrong end of the stick! Saint Bernard, reduced to a few hectares!

Saint Bernard founded Claraval (1115), a place his name would be associated with. It had been preceded by

La Ferté (1113), Pontigny (1114), Morimond (1115). It seems incredible, but is absolutely true. By the end of that century five hundred and thirty Cistercian monasteries had sprung up all over Europe. There were seven hundred by the 17th Century. The founding of three hundred and fifty is attributed to Saint Bernard. It is incredible, no *mass media, no marketing*[T.N.], no communications media, no transport. A chain reaction from France through Spain and Portugal, to England and Ireland, the Netherlands and Germany, to Italy, Hungary, Croatia, Poland and the Scandinavian kingdoms, etc. Besides a pleiad of saints, the New Order also spawned spiritual writers who are still a delight. E. Gilson remarks that the Cistercians had relinquished everything but the art of good writing. So many hidden or overlooked treasures! Every year I long for the day when it is the turn of Aelredo de Rieval and Isaac de Stella to appear in the breviary readings, to say nothing of William of Saint Thierry and Guerrico d'Igny. They are specialists of the spirit, soul-miners, pot-holers of the heart, forgotten by westerners of today, who, famished and anxious, merely drink from far-off and exotic fonts and Eastern gurus.

Zacarías could hardly have known any of this the day his trembling hand eventually mustered up the courage to knock the handle of the front door of La Oliva, his heart beating heavily in his breast! All he knew was that he wanted to become a convert brother... Without a shadow of a doubt!

[T.N.] These words appear thus in the original Spanish, in italics.

III
WHAT IS A CONVERT BROTHER?

In his lovely book, the *Cistercian Way*, André Louf says that in the epoch immediately after the Second Vatican Council, amid the fever and the uncertainty with which the religious orders and congregations sought renovation, there was one word constantly on the lips of all monks, which sounded like an ancient maxim:

> "A brother asks an ancient: What is a monk?"
>
> And the ancient replied: "The monk is he who wonders every day: What is a monk?"

The thing has more substance than it seems to, but we shall have to forget it for the moment, because in all probability it did not trouble Zacarías when he entered La Oliva. Onofre would have explained to him that he was going to work in the monastery, more or less as he had done in Oteiza, but this time with a meaning and a horizon to look to. Therein lay the mysterious and fundamental difference. Perhaps he really had no proper idea of what a convert brother was.

Just at the outset of the 12th Century, the so-called *Exordio parvo* (1120), chap. XVI, talks about the Order's determination to receive "bearded lay converts", and treat them, in life and in death, like monks. They were not monks in the strict sense of the word. They governed the agricultural lands of the monastery, although they were not really a novelty. They had already appeared as far back as the 9th Century among the Benedictines, who called them lay servers, familiars or serfs. The formula was followed in the 11th Century by Saint Romuald in Camaldule, by Saint John Gualbert, by the Carthusians. They were helpers of the monks, basic pieces for the monasteries to be able to subsist. In the Cistercian order they acquired a fixed status. They took vows as converts. They looked after the farms belonging to the monastery, near and far. They were able to leave the monastery, talk, have contact with the outside world.

Following the Council, things changed a great deal and we must fast-forward to the thirties to get a glimpse of Zacarías' real life. One monk actually warned me and provided me with reading material that proved to be fundamental: *Uses of the Convert Brethren of the Cistercian Order from the Rule of Saint Benedict and the Constitutions of the Order*, *published by the General Chapter of 1927*. Burgos, typeface of "El Monte Carmelo", 1931, 352 pp.

On March 21, 1928, the Order dated the Preface of the work in Rome:

> *"Saint Alberic, the second Abbot of the Cistercian order, prescribed the admission of convert brethren, i.e. lay brethren or coadjutors, who would be specially dedicated to manual work. Thanks to this determination the choir monks could apply themselves to singing the Holy Office with greater solemnity and devote more time to spiritual exercises. The great Exordium of the Cistercian order, the Menology of the Order and the Annals of the Trappe mention the innumerable convert*

brethren who were excellent models of all monastic virtues and who reached great holiness.

Veritable monks in all senses of the word, convert brethren, however, are not actually monks, as they do not serve in the choir, and neither do they have an active or passive voice, to wit, they can neither choose nor be chosen or take part in the administration and governance of the monastery.

Veritable members of the Order and the community, their life, one of great sacrifice, silence and prayer, is intimately linked to that of the Fathers. They are brethren of the choir monks, and as such must care for and may share all their belongings. According to an old Cistercian prescription, they are to be treated as choir monks in life and in death. They both pursue the same ideal, to wit, the perfection of spiritual life via reflection and penitence, and all of them, united as one, follow the same Rule, that of Saint Benedict."

Indeed, this preface is followed by the Rule of Saint Benedict, the Constitutions of the Order and strict observance approved and confirmed by the Holy See in 1925.

In chapter VII of part three thereof, reference is made to the convert brethren, and they will help us to trace the steps followed by Zacarías following his arrival at the monastery.

He would have begun with six months as a postulant before being admitted to the Novitiate. Following eight full days of spiritual exercises, the postulants wore the novice's habit and began the novitiate period, which lasted two years. After this they took their simple vows, which were for three years. Following this period they could be admitted to take their perpetual solemn vows. Throughout this time they were to observe the rules of the monks. Their brown woollen habit consisted of a tunic, scapular, leather girdle and cloak. Those received as convert brethren, who would never become choir singers or choir men, attended Mass on feasts of the saints and Conventual Vespers. Their time was devoted to work, which they would take to on normal days after mental prayer and private Mass. They did not pray the Holy Office, but honours established in the Cistercian Ritual. Some priest monks heard their confession: one, who was known as the Convert Brother Master, taught them the Christian doctrine and the Rule. They ate at the common table, but only observed the common fasts of the Church. Their free time was spent in prayer or pious reading, although not in the cloister with the monks, but separately.

Nevertheless, the main course of the book in question is that which is titled *Uses of the Convert Brethren of the Cistercian Order of Strict Observance*. It comprises eleven books with numerous chapters, which establish the uses in the reception of the Brothers, the order of their Exercises, ceremonies in general, regular Offices, the celebration of Masses, feasts of the saints in the year, monastic observances, regular places, uses with the sick and the deceased, special tasks, etc… We can safely say that all these norms configured the life of Zacarías.

For some days, as a postulant, he was accommodated in the guest house, where he would seek to discover whether the spirit of God was leading him to embrace that life, and here he would be questioned by the Superior. He would make up the list of the belongings that he had brought: his soldier's uniform and little else. On entering the community he would faithfully follow the exercises of the convert brethren. He would receive his habits after six months of postulancy:

"What do you wish?"

"The mercy of God and of the Order."

Following the relevant exhortation by the Superior, and on being asked if he was prepared to follow the Rule and persevere in his new vocation, he would reply:

– Yes, Reverent Father, with the grace of God and the succour of your prayers."

The ceremony would conclude with a thanksgiving in the temple.

That day heralded the beginning of his novitiate. Zacarías, who had been an Oblate since September 16, 1928, began his novitiate on March 10, 1929. For two years, separated from the monks, he would apply himself fully to learning his obligations, and attend the talks given by the novice Master. At the end of this two-year period, if deemed worthy, he would be admitted to the faith. He would first take his temporary vows, receive his monk's habit, and have his head shaved. Zacarías made his temporary profession of faith on March 19, 1931. Three years later he would be entitled to take his solemn vows, after giving up his worldly possessions and eight full days of Exercises. On the eve of his ceremony he would write, in his own hand:

I, brother Zacarías Santamaría Aramendia, a convert brother, vow stability, conversion of customs and obedience according to the Rule of Saint Benedict Abbot, before God and his saints, whose relics are venerated here in this monastery of Santa María de la Oliva of the Cistercian Order of Strict Observance, built in honour of the Blessed Mary, the Mother of God and Virgin, in the presence of the Abbot of this monastery."

Following the vow of stability, he would read the certificate of his profession and present it to the Abbot, who would give him the kiss of peace, and he would lie on the floor as the community sang the Miserere Psalm. He would then take his seat in the choir and take communion that day at High Mass. This all came to pass on March 19, 1934.

The vow of stability bound him to Santa María de la Oliva forever. Only a written order from his Abbot would suffice for him to change home. Those stout walls would be his mansion for life.

Stability... and conversion of customs, the finality and *raison d'être* of that decisive change. And with stability in space came another type of stability, or setting of hours, in time. Everything pre-established, in winter and summer alike, or in liturgical times such as Lent, the holy triduo, fasts, etc... The year would contain more working days than holidays.

What was a day in La Oliva like, a normal working day in summer, for a convert brother?

2 am Rise and prayer.

3 am Mass of the Holy Virgin, praying of the Prime in the choir stall, make bed, mixed, work.

9.45 am Tierce

10.45 am Sext and examination.

11 am Lunch. Thanksgiving. Angelus. Clear the table. Midday Nap.

1 pm End of midday nap. None. Reception. Interval.

1.45 pm Wash the dishes. Work.

5 pm Vespers.

5.30 pm End of work. Interval.

6 pm Supper. Clear the table and wash the dishes. Interval.

7.10 pm Reading.

8 pm Bedtime

And so on, for twenty, thirty, fifty years, according to the will of the Lord.

Not only in space and time. Everything in monastery life is regulated for monks and convert brethren: they way they enter and exit the church, the different postures to be adopted in the different services, their place… The timetable refers to an *interval*. Well, the brethren could go to the church during all the intervals, albeit without neglecting their obligatory reading, and nor could they sit down; they were to pray either standing up or kneeling down. Many of them recall the figure of Zacarías praying on his knees, almost curled up, or hunched on his heels.

The brethren were obliged to carry out other offices or prayers other than those of the choir. The Office of the Our Father, the so-called De Betate Virgine, the deceased, prayers for deceased Fathers and Brethren, or for dead guests and familiars. They only said them in the choir on Sundays and holidays, although everyone did so separately. On working days, which were the majority, only the Matins, Lauds, Prime and Compline were said in the choir.

The Uses meticulously describe the minimum details of each one of these prayers, as well as that of the Salve that brings the day to a close after the Compline. Having sung the Salve, "at the Superior's sign they get up, bow deeply towards the altar and as they leave the church also bow before the Superior to receive the holy water, whereupon they cover themselves and withdraw to their dormitories."

Yes, I am sure, on the afternoon on which I write, that the ritual in which I have sometimes participated will take place at the exact time. The finishing touch of the Salve, with the temple dark and the Holy Mary of La Oliva illuminated by a powerful and exact white spotlight, in unforgettable. And almost equally unforgettable is the triple pealing of the bell, tolled by one of the Brethren in full view, counterpoint to the heavy silence of the night and precedes the silent procession of the Brethren past the Abbot to be blessed with the holy water. The day's film is over, yet another day devoted to the Lord, and in his presence… Then…

Silence!… and… cut. The only action will be that of the day.

Profound, average or slight inclination, arms hanging or crossed over the chest, prostration on the knuckles, ways of kneeling and sitting, etc… everything is measured and regulated. Some may see this as an affront to personal freedom. They are simple family gestures which are slowly but surely assimilated, becoming part of the nature. Once they have been interiorised… they help to place body and soul in the trance of prayer. "All prayer" –as is stated in book four– chapter 1 –"must be said with respect, attention and devotion, three words that clearly indicate that man must contribute with his body, spirit and heart to the fulfilment of such a sacred duty." Naturally, body, spirit and heart: everything is permeated by the thought of being before God. This is why great attention must be paid to the words spoken, and how they are spoken. And above all attention to God, the object of prayer. It is the effort to adjust our whole being for it to seek the harmony with which the Other One surrounds and transcends us. This is the school in which the spirit of Brother Zacarías was modelled.

But there is more, much more. I cannot go into it all, although I would like to address some aspects that have a special impact on his life. And they should not be forgotten, because they will emerge later. The figure of the Abbot is important in the monastery. Book VII, On monastic observances, contains a choice instruction, which affords meaning to the meticulous practices that are later described, and which we are going to leave aside:

> *"The duty of the Abbot is not only to govern the monastery on the outside, but even more so it is to lead the souls entrusted to him along the paths to perfection. As father of the spiritual family he will enjoy the utmost confidence of the brethren. The solicitous monk*

concerned about the good of his soul will hide nothing from him, will bare his innermost soul to him, the goodness residing therein, and even any ill disposition that might perturb his peace and serenity."

n.204 The convert brethren will neither do nor undertake anything without the order or permission of the Superior."

Can you now glimpse why, in the form of the little bird, Zacarías flew, at his own funeral, to the shoulder of the Abbot? He did not wish to undertake the final flight without the order or permission of his Superior. It was the parting gesture of one whose life had been governed by this principle.

Secondly, Cistercian life is coenobitic, to wit community-based, and to what an extent! Community in the church, at work, in the refectory, in hours devoted to study or reading in the great common room, and even in the dormitory. In this last regard the amendments introduced after the Second Vatican Council changed things. They now have individual cells to sleep in, although at that time they used to sleep in the common dormitory, separated by small partitions. I was shown one such L-shaped room in the old rooms of the monastery, which are no longer used, and where the community slept together for many years. They told me that one of the rooms was used for those who snored, which they had dubbed "the orchestra room". Imagine the snores of those of peaceful soul and tired body after the day's hard work! And this was not the only penitence reserved for the scant hours of sleep, which were interrupted by Matins. Until not so long ago the brethren used to sleep with their habit on, which they had worn over a long and hard day's work in the fields. If the snores were anything but celestial, then the odours pervading the room would have at least equalled them.

Hours of sleep were scarce, more time was spent in coexistence with the community, awake. Here the golden rule comes from Saint Paul: "Love each other as brothers, care for and honour one another." This translates into respect, love, obedience and mutual service." Taking nothing, they never give what is "mine", but rather "ours", "our book", "our habit", but they will not say "our head", "our hand" or "we have done", as is provided for by no. 208 of the Uses.

The outside bearing, that sort of halo that surrounds the figure of the monk, is the fruit of his severe discipline, of a taming of the body. Not the violent and harsh taming the athlete undergoes through long training, but rather a subtle operation that gradually converts the body into a receiver and a transmitter of spirit, a transparent case of the soul housed within. Chapter VIII, no. III addresses the Uses:

> *"The brethren must always observe the utmost humility, walk without haste and without looking round, keep themselves clean, avoiding any illness, and taking due care of their habits and everything they have for their use... They will kiss the cloak and chaperon before donning them." (No. 209)*

In this world of vertigo and stress, the monk, also the convert brother, walks without haste, as if he had already settled in eternity. What need is there to hurry or make haste? Does the Gospel not say that every day has its weight (Matthew 6, 34). It is a man who looks inwards. All that is outside him, even the limited outside of his life, is accidental.

Here we must address the question of silence, which is emphasised in the Uses:

> *"Saint Benedict understood that the monk must be mainly a man of prayer, he knew very well that the most propitious medium to facilitate the practice of inner life is silence. And that is why he frequently recommends that his disciples keep silence faithfully. Our fathers of the Cistercian Order, strict observers of all the points of the Rule, also strived to keep this one, which, so to speak, they converted into the soul of our monastic observances."*

Consequently, no. 216 of the Uses prescribes: *"The brethren will not communicate with each other by word or in writing. When they have to communicate they will do so by signs."* This general monastic rule could only be broken by the convert brethren to talk to the Abbot, the novice Master or the Cellarer for the purpose of work. The strictest silence, from the afternoon Angelus to the Prime the following morning, prevailed, and could only be broken in the case of emergency. Moreover, this obligatory silence affected not only speaking, but also shouting, making noise on opening and closing doors, or when walking. Nothing was to perturb the tranquillity of the monastery.

We have been told that silence is the "soul" of monastic observance. As I am also told, the observance of this precept was strict until recently. The monastery brethren still recall the story of two brethren –blood brethren– who lived there for many years and never uttered a word to each other, communicating by signs only.

The Book of Uses contains an extensive code of the signs the monks used to communicate. Zacarías taught some convert brethren this code.

Sleep: nod the head on top of the hand.

Incarnate: Place finger tip on bottom lip.

Salad: The sign for grass (move one hand and then the other, stretched out in parallel) and vinegar (place the tip of the index finger on the tip of the nose and scratch the throat from chin to gullet.

Bury: the sign for the spade (move feet and hands in digging movement) and death (thumb under the chin, lifting the fist).

Elderly: The signs for the year (stretching the left arm and touching the shoulder with the right hand) and the sign for very much (draw a line from one shoulder to the other) and the sign for the person.

The day before yesterday: Twice the sign for yesterday (move fist towards the shoulder).

Angel: The signs of the wing (place the tip of the thumb on the angle of the mouth, stretching out the hand and moving it).

The chapter on "How to make signs" spans no less than 36 pages. Throughout the best part of his life, Zacarías observed these rules scrupulously, although sometimes his post as cellarer allowed him –and obliged him– to talk to the people who worked in the monastery. Nevertheless, and even after this practice was suppressed in more recent times, he was never a great talker. He used words sparingly, and would not use five words if three sufficed.

Let us now leave aside everything pertaining to private reading, chapter of sins, penitence, etc.... but not matters pertaining to food, since it should be known that "the use of meat, fish and eggs is forbidden to sections of the community" (no. 264). Butter and oil are permitted as seasoning. Rice. Legumes, pasta, roots are the base of the monk's diet. Dessert was fruit, fresh or uncooked, honey, radish. The best bread was served to the sick, and the normal bread, a mixture of rye or other grains, was for the community. Potatoes could be added to bread, except on Good Friday, which was a day of strict fasting on bread and water.

Two cooked portions are served with meals, with soup counted as one portion. Two portions are served with the evening meal, one of which may be cheese. Eating is not permitted outside the refectory. Monks and convert brethren partake of the same food, and the common drink of the country is served in the refectory. The light meal consists of six ounces of bread and eight ounces of a dessert or salad. By virtue of their stiffer work the convert brethren could request the so-called alleviation, i.e. an extra portion, also of milk and eggs, at any time, even on Fridays in Lent.

The Cellarer was responsible for the food of the Community and how it was cooked. Far be it for me to go into the nutritional virtues of the diet –many monks reach healthy old age on it– and its possible untoward consequences. José told me in confidence that the his brother Zacarías' stomach deteriorated quickly, and for good.

And now we come to another chapter essential in understanding the life of Zacarías; work. If silence is the "soul" of monastic life, then work is the body, at least as far as the convert brethren are concerned, who for years now have worn full beard (no. 294). Yes, it is true that there was a Room for the convert brethren where they did all their reading. There was a drawer under the seat for them to stash the books they read. The were also addressed by the Abbot in that room, which harboured the brethren's "common box", with its hidden treasures, such as pen and ink, yarn, needles, scissors, pins, but no long etcetera that would give rise to *embarrass du choix*.

But the brethren's veritable room was the field, their corn fields, vegetable gardens and orchards. Work was their mainstay, the equilibrium of mental and physical effort. Indeed, shortly after the foundation of the Cistercian Order, The Blessed Guerric d'Igny would write: "*Work is like the ballast that balances the vessel, it is a weight that affords rest and stability to worried hearts, and sets man's inner self in order.*" Every day the cellarer would punctually allocate the tasks to the brethren, as well as the tool needed to carry it out, hoe, pruning shears, saw, basket etc…

There were three jobs which could be defined as specific, and which Zacarías would perform in succession: work in the field, the kitchen and the door.

The countryside surrounding the monastery: wheat and cornfields with their stages of sowing, tending and harvesting, the orchard and vegetable garden with greens and fruits. There was a time when seasonal hands were taken on to help with the harvesting. This was all managed by the Cellarer. The actual word appears in the Uses and has a certain charm. It comes from the Latin word *cella*, the chamber where the wheat or tithes or income were collected; the person in charge was the *cellarer*. A brother with the title of subcellarer could replace the cellarer if the latter was absent. The cellarer is a fundamental part of the monastery, along with the Abbot and the Novice Master. He was responsible for organising work, the economy and the material subsistence of the monastery.

The kitchen was another crucial place, however elementary the fare may have been. Nobody could enter the kitchen without permission except the cellarer, the guest house keeper and the nurse. Can you imagine a room next to the kitchen, pompously called the "laboratory"? It has nothing to do with the modern meaning of the word, and neither should we think that delicate or sophisticated dishes were cooked up in there. It was simply the place of work –labour, *laboratorium*, just like the *scriptorium* was where they wrote. The laboratory where vegetables were prepared for meals. Spick and span, where the utmost silence prevailed. The only talking allowed there was for work (no. 319). A third job for the brethren is that of the porter, at the door, where visitors or occasional guests arrived. The brethren must welcome them kindly, with talking kept to the purely indispensable. We might also mention the job of sub-nurse and finally that of sub-housekeeper, who replaced the housekeeper when the latter was at choir, and also attended to guests, cleaned their rooms, clothes or shoes, and was, in a few words, to "attend to them in accordance with the dictates of charity and good manners."

The foregoing will serve to give us an overview of the framework in which the best part of Zacarías' life unfolded, a modest map of his movements inside the monastery, his path over the years, rather monotonous and unchanging. Do you ever have the sensation, when walking over a beauty spot or contemplating scenery, that you have been there before with a loved one or someone who is no longer with you? I will always remember my excursions in the mountains of Riglos with my elderly parents and the photos we took on the road next to the vineyard of Olite.

We came past here –I say to myself–, we took in this same view... Here, here, but that is a schematic and poor piece of information: the materiality of a plot of land, bereft of other singular complements. What about the time of day, or night, the temperature, our state of joy or sadness, that vital moment... the time, which is unique and will never happen again, we passed through here? We retain virtually nothing of it. In our case we would have to look upon that confined little space with the eyes of, or rather *from the soul of Zacarías*.

We have made a stop in the vital framework of space and time, the occupations of Zacarías. Can we now peer into his innermost mystery?

Well, before attempting to do so, I must make one further point. A few lines above I wrote that "the best part" of Zacarías' life unfolded in this framework. But why not say "all" of it? Because there is a fundamental dividing line, namely the year 1965. A year that culminated in a process of innovation of the Order which gave rise to the Decree of the Holy Congregation of the Religious (December 27, 1965). This decree suppressed the original and lay figure of the convert brother.

As of that moment there was only one class of religious person in the Order, they were all monks, with the same monastic training and the same rights and duties. Therefore the only distinctions between them were imposed by the different occupations to which monks are devoted, taking the special vocation of God and personal attitudes into account. The Liturgy was imposed on all of them as an essential element of their life.

As of that moment convert brothers were part of the choir, they were real monks. The Revolutionary Decree left a little door open: Those who had taken their vows as convert brothers could continue to practice as such. They would be extinguished when the last of their kind died.

Shall I add that some modern monks feel a certain nostalgia for the convert brothers, for the great examples of holiness that many of them showed? For the sake of modernity, the suppression of class differences, the convert brothers disappeared. As if there were classes of holiness or saintliness, and as if the simplest convert brother could not be holier than the Abbot himself! Some of them live on as myths. Oh for those convert brothers, giants of the spirit! says one monk. And Zacarías was one of them from 1929 until 1965, and continued to be so in his heart, regardless of amendments.

The Australian chaffinch appeared in San Sebastián

IV
ZACARÍAS, THE CONVERT BROTHER

He knocked at the door, still in his soldier's garb, crossed the threshold and entered the new world he had dreamed of. The mandatory days in the guest house went by, and he opened his soul to the Superior and to the Padre Maestro, he gave up the few belongings that he had, writing a double list of them, one for him and one for the Padre Maestro. What belongings would he have, other than his torn soldier's uniform? He started to follow the habitual exercises of the community, always in front of the latest novice. His period as a postulant lasted six months, enough for him to understand the rigours of what his new life was to be.

That strong, weather-beaten young man gave himself up generously to the new discipline: imposed but embraced. In less than two years his health had gone forever. There have been sick saints. Saint Ignatius was one of them, and he confessed that when a servant of the Lord emerges from sickness, he does so as "half doctor". Zacarías became a fully-fledged doctor.

Once he told brother José, my informant, that it was all due to the food at the monastery. "That "pigswill" they serve for breakfast," he would say. He would eat it with enormous disgust, equalled only by his spirit of obedience. His stomach put up with anything and everything, with tremendous ulcers as its only reward. The lack of hygiene would have had less effect on the young man from Oteiza: from prayer to the fields in a sweat-soaked habit, from grim heat to cool temple. The first years in La Oliva were of dreadful, almost subhuman, austerity. Some vocations lilted under such pressure, but Zacarías held out, his body putting up with the punishment.

Was it when he took his orders, his admission to the novitiate, into the profession? His brother Joseph assures me that at one of those crucial moments –probably the third– the community, summoned by the Superior for that very purpose, raised doubts as to his admission. Some withheld their vote for the sick young man, who lacked the health needed to withstand full and regular observance. Others defended his admission, alleging that despite his poor health his conduct was faultless, perfect, observant, industrious, spiritual... He was eventually admitted, and was destined to become the most esteemed, appreciated and the best-known person in the monastery. We know nothing of his spiritual tribulations at that difficult time. His understandable concern would later give way to peace.

Two or three years after his admission, he was visited by his brother José, who was studying Humanities and Philosophy at the Claretian Seminary of Beire. He vividly remembers the afternoon that lecturers and students went to visit the monastery. It was the first time he had seen his brother as a monk. Having secured the Superior's permission, Zacarías went out to welcome them. They visited the temple, the monastery and cellars and other rooms. It was in the month of May. He still remembers that they did the flower exercises and sang the Ave Maria by the Claretian F. Iruarrizaga. A great composer –may I say– who died the very day I was born. José emotionally recalled how the visiting seminarians never left Zacarías' side. They were greatly impressed and touched by that affectionate and kind brother, so full of God. They all said that he looked like a Saint and that was all they talked about on the way back. The spiritual Father who accompanied them attempted to play down their enthusiasm: "Brother Zacarías is a Convert Brother who has only been in the monastery for a few years. God tends to imbue new converts with great fervour, thus enabling them to start their new spiritual life with a flourish. As the years go by, this fervour tends to wane, and the monk returns to a normal and peaceful life."

The principle may be correct, although the application thereof or the prophecy were not. Zacarías' initial fervour never waned, but increased throughout his life, as all those who had dealings with him will bear witness to. And his face, the mirror of his soul, illuminated by a strange permanent smile, even then, and until is death, was like an open window onto an indefinable inner mystery.

We have mentioned his chronic stomach pains, and neither may we forget another constant physical complaint. I could not say when it started, although I do know that for many years Zacarías had to sleep sitting up or in an armchair in the infirmary, as an asthma condition made it impossible for him to sleep lying down in the hard old bed of the dormitory. This was an additional trial over and above the already scant hours of sleep the Cistercians had. He never spoke of his pains or complaints, he simply bore them in silence and looked upon them as a penitence.

What is more, they cannot be overlooked if we wish to delve further into the profound mystery of his soul. In the symphony of his life, disease is like the pipe part of the bagpipe, giving it those constant deep tones over which the melodies are built. Stomach complaint, asthma, the last disease: he accepted everything with love, as if it had been thus provided for by the hand of God, one monk told me.

This is the framework of Zacarías' life, that of the Cistercian monk. You might say to me, well that is the theory, the principle, the ideal, and that there is always a difference between what is promised and what is delivered. Do we not often hear of tight airline schedules that are never met, election promises that nobody ever intends to keep anyway? Our case is different, particularly bearing in mind the rigour that prevailed in La Oliva at the time. Beginning with the strict timetable, we may say that it marked, unfailingly, all the hours of his life. And ditto the rhythmic intermittence of prayer and work. The Abbot Mariano, who had more dealings with him than anyone, told me that *"he was always where he was supposed to be, and went unnoticed in the life of the community, never asking for anything"*. Like the natural routine of dawn and sunset, heat in summer and cold in winter. What marvellous praise!

Having said this, the foregoing is but the shell of his life, the bark of the tree, something that may be fulfilled by an outer appearance that might harbour different inner feelings. Can we ever glimpse the hidden secret of such a life? And the poet Gonzalo de Berceo said:

Let us cut away the outside, and enter the heart,

At least as best we can.

MY FOLDER

His life, his days, were meticulously programmed. It was enclosed, reduced to a limited space: temple, refectory, field, kitchen, door. The only silent witnesses of his life were those who lived with him. In the part of his life that unfolded at the doorway he was seen by and had doings with those who approached it. Who, how many, how would he deal with them? Only the monks can help me to unravel the life of Zacarías. And to them I went for them to confide their news and impressions in me.

My folder contains their answers, and before proceeding we must stop to reflect. I told the monks that I did not need to know their names, but I did want to know for how long they had lived with Zacarías in the monastery. My request overwhelmed the limits of the monastery and even reached those who had lived there for a while but who had left it. Some of them had stayed there for fifteen months, others three years, quite a few twenty, and the odd monk more than forty. Like Zacarías, they also looked more into themselves than at what was going on around them, and observed the obligatory silence which was hardly conducive to intimate communication and effusion. But when all is said and done, monks also have eyes to contemplate life, and life brings them together in shared places. They saw the shell of Zacarías' life, and their perspicacity in turn may give us an insight into his spirit. They offered me their impressions generously, sometimes in the form of anecdotes like little wild flowers that we gather in the countryside. Brothers or convert brothers –I make no distinction– sometimes bearers of names that seem to come from a Medieval cartulary: Gracilano, Ventura, Mariano, Manuel, Luis Alfonso, Jeremías, Hermenegildo, Vicente, Florencio, Sotero, etc…

I have also been aided by people who looked after Zacarías during his stays in the Hospital of Pamplona for his illnesses and operations, and who enthusiastically recall vivid, humane and edifying anecdotes. Pilar and Júlia, the latter a daughter of the Alfaro couple that brought up José.

So perhaps this will suffice to make up a humble bouquet of flowers, a few brushstrokes that will allow us to glimpse part of the mystery of the life of Zacarías.

V
FROM THE OUTSIDE

They walk together, barely talking, along the same path, with shared desires. Even at night, the mere fact of walking together, something, and more than something, must make its way to the surface; if the companion puffs or pants or walks at a brisk pace, if he lags or always takes the lead, if he walks with determination or as if tired. I am referring to the monks, or the monks of La Oliva. Having lived together for more or fewer years, what would they have seen in Zacarías?

In some cases, fifteen months of coexistence in the monastery with him sufficed to make a deep mark in one:

> *"I did the washing, and sometimes I had to go to the front door to put out the empty butane gas cylinder and pick up the new full one"*, spoke one who had left the monastery. *"Several times, three of four perhaps, I made the most of the opportunity to chat to Brother Zacarías. I was irresistibly drawn by his mystery. I wanted to listen him and also question him, with picaresque devotion. I would entice him into conversation, try to get him to talk about himself, reveal something, anything, to gain an inkling as to that unfathomable mystery, an insight into Zacarías, that volcano of love of God and men. I felt a sort of vertigo in the presence of that old monk, on daring to approach him and talk to him. He would receive me with the utmost simplicity, with true sincerity and charity,*

veritable affection. Never once did I perceive unease, strain or impatience in him on being interrupted by a novice like myself.

I have three letters from him which I deeply treasure. There is one in which he says to me: "And now my dear Father, I offer my poor prayers to you, and you may be sure that I will be with you always, and you know that I pray constantly. He was always available, close, pleasant. He appreciated, as a saint can, my status as a priest, but treated me simply and warmly, and that spurred me on to act simply and transparently with him, like a true friend, like a brother.

He was sad and disappointed when I left the monastery; he wrote a harsh letter to me: "You tricked me like a child," he wrote. For me he was the maestro, the oracle, the man of God. For me it was by the grace of God and a privilege to be able to talk to that man, get so close to him. From the laundry room I would watch him repair to sing the Sext, praying with his Rosary as he went. I delighted in seeing him and stopped to watch him walk along the path, and was even more delighted when he was by my side, singing Lauds. I was the last priest and he was the first monk in seniority.

When I left the monastery, a novice at the time, he called me a coward and said that I was weak:

"Let me get it off my chest, because I love you so much that it is beyond your comprehension."

I discovered that my path had to be different, although I believe that he died with the conviction that I was wrong, even although in his last two letters he seemed to have calmed down, and he gave me advice for my life as a minister and on how to overcome the difficulties that life held and how to deal with the men I would have to live with. I think that he will have understood me, in Heaven. Many a time do I call on him, I have asked for his advice, I have felt his presence and his influence, I feel that he still loves me."

Another who lived with Zacarías for the last three years of his life defined him as "a perfect model of a convert brother", with his innate and unmistakeable spirituality. Such was the mark that Zacarías' example made on him that he desired to follow in his footsteps. That was when this class was suppressed in the Order. He once mentioned his vocation to be a convert brother to Zacarías, and how the novice Master had refused to admit him, as it was a thing of the past. Zacarías told him: *"It is a beautiful vocation. However, even if there are now only monks, you can always be a monk that prays a lot, works hard, austere, which is what the convert brother does. Follow the advice of your Master Father."* He did just that, although he always felt called upon to be a convert brother. He never forgot the teachings of Zacarías, and is convinced that the most beautiful pages of the Cistercian history were written by the convert brethren.

One of my other informants did not get past the postulant stage, lasting but a few months. This took place four years before the death of Zacarías. He had dealings and talked to him in the kitchen, and later visited him after leaving the monastery. He recalls him as a *servant of God, a friend, a brother*:

"When I started in the kitchen Zacarías was already famous for his saintly ways. But what is a saint?

I know not. All I can say is that brother Zacarías was a man of God, one who was blessed, a son of Mary. He pronounced the name of God in a whisper. He would say Jesus with the utmost love, and it was this love that made him live and afforded him his ardent fervour. One day, in his own way he explained the mystery of the Holy Trinity to me. He told me that it was the love between Father and Son that engendered the Holy Spirit. He loved the Virgin and told me of the power of her love. Once he told me that the Devil was like a tied-up dog, but that we had Mary and as long as we were in her arms he could do us no evil, and that there was nothing to fear from him. One day I asked him what the most difficult part of life in the monastery was for him, and he answered without hesitating: obedience. Later I learnt that he had once worn a shaggy beard which he was ordered to shave off, which hurt him.

He liked to go unnoticed, and did not like to be tightly embraced by people, saying that such embraces were like a bath by the Holy Ghost; or that someone, on seeing him enter the kitchen, would shout his name out. His life was poor and humble in the extreme. He would always strive to economise for the sake of the community, by peeling the skin of potatoes as thin as possible, or wearing old and torn gloves. One day, when I was a postulant, I saw him in the washing room after lunch, with his torn gloves, and volunteered to help him. He declined, with that angelical smile he always had. All I remember is that later, when I went up to the novitiate, I felt a sensation of peace and plenitude that lasted some time. I also remember that Zacarías appreciated purity, and he often told me that there was nothing more beauteous than a pure and chaste young man.

"I never saw him angry, he was always smiling, evincing great spiritual humility. He always sought to be the last. He was very observant of Uses and Rules," told me another man who spent four years alongside him.

In photography, exposure is the time that the lens remains open to capture the image better. So, on an ascending time scale, we shall pass on to the witnesses to whom Zacarías was "exposed" longer. They were with him for longer and will allow us to retrieve some further-off memories, even going back as far his youth.

Thus, some who had spent little more than seven years with Zacarías can give us an insight into Zacarías' earlier life, referring to a profound change that sparked his vocation, and above all his radical way of living that vocation. How could I have learnt that Zacarías was a rather mischievous adolescent, the leader of the brawls between the young lads of Oteiza in the *fiestas* of the neighbouring villages? He confesses to having heard people give voice to utterances such as "He's a right one is that boy", or "You should have seen him when he was a boy!" And naturally there was always someone around to remember how a group of young boys –including Zacarías– got up to some mischief which went too far, leading the Mayor and the Civil Guard to intervene. Zacarías, the ringleader, persuaded them all to keep mum, thinking that such a course of action would get them out of the predicament, and it did.

The same informant also knew something about Zacarías' girlfriend, before he joined the Order, and knew even more about what happened later, the unusual and moving story of the would-be girlfriend: "She went to see him every year, and continued to do so even after she got married, accompanied by her husband and children. The children really loved him. I personally remember how they went to visit him when he was in hospital with their own families. And before that, when she fell seriously ill, her husband petitioned the Abbot to allow Zacarías to go to Pamplona, because his wife wanted to take her leave of Zacarías before she died." And he went there, in the company of the Abbot. "Seeing their holy embrace was an emotional experience" says my informant.

It seems like a story taken from an old Chronicle: Saint Benedict and Santa Escolástica, Saint Francis and Saint Claire. We must go back to it.

The episodes we have already heard are but wood chippings from a statue. Let us take a closer look at the actual statue, because, in the words of our witness:

> *He was a man of great prayer, which was evident in his demeanour. This, besides his peculiar and constant smile, attracted people's attention in a very special way. Many people, who neither knew him nor had ever had any dealings with him, simply on seeing him at church, would ask, out of curiosity and interest, who the white-haired monk with the special smile was, and would express their desire to talk to him.*
>
> *When I was still in the guest house, I realised, somewhat to my surprise, that anyone who talked to him was charmed and captivated. And the strange thing is that he was a man of few words who would speak only when spoken to.*

He was very diligent in the tasks entrusted to him and was very punctual. I knew him as a porter and kitchen assistant. On one occasion, when he was left alone for a few months, he expressed his concern as to whether his meals were good or whether he was giving his fellow monks a hard time of it. When he was on the door, he would say the rosary when he had nothing to do, and as soon as the bells started to peal to signal the end of work, he would stop on the spot, head between his hands, and would pray, as long as no one came, until the bells called the brethren to Vespers.

Luis Alfonso is now a happy father. While still young, and alone in life, he frequently sought succour in La Oliva, and there he met Zacarías, who was in charge of the guest house. On certain occasions, the Superior, fed up of seeing the boy there, told Zacarías that he did not want to sec him around the monastery again. But Zacarías, who was fully aware of the boy's plight, homeless and destitute, allowed him to come back. The boy never forgot that. He made it through those trying times thanks to the monastery, and to Zacarías. *"Brother Zacarías"* –he writes, *"was extremely patient with me, always treated me like a son, and never once did he frown upon my frequent visits. Who knows what would have become of me had it not been for the help and affection he bestowed upon me. I trust that he will always be my defender and that he shall open the eternal door of the guest house to me for us both to live in happiness with Our Lord."*

After twenty years together –from 1966 until 1986– another brother recalls him as "a very spiritual monk, simple and full of goodness", and adds:

"It was evident that he reached the highest level of union with God, and that his life was one of frequent prayer, if not constant. Besides the Hours of the Office, he would also pray in the church, and outside it, with his rosary between his hands.

He faithfully observed the acts of community life and was diligent and responsible in carrying out his tasks, as porter and later as kitchen assistant. He was very affectionate towards the brethren and anyone that came to the monastery. He was serene and of a gentle smile, he spoke little but always to the point, and brimmed with spirituality, he was always willing to help. Everyone that knew him loved him, and many people found edification in him. He prayed a lot for the salvation of souls and for the Church to prosper... All that I know of his life before the monastery was that he said he had been a great sinner in his youth.

Those who had known Zacarías for longer allow us to salvage more of his life.

Some suggested that I ask Hermenegildo, who was in Rome at the General Curia of the Order.

I wanted to talk to Hermenegildo personally, and actually spoke to him on the phone. The day we were due to meet there was a bus strike in Rome, and he lived far away, a good few kilometres away from the Centre. I wrote him a letter and he very kindly answered. His letter surprised me. Who would ever have imagined? He had lived with Zacarías since 1948, but had very seldom spoken to him. "Both of us had been trained in the strict observance of silence. We were used to that, to simply greeting each other with a smile. Moreover, I am not very observant."

Even so, that rather unobservant man made a general *observation* that should be taken into account:

"I feel it is important to frame the life of this monk in the environment he lived in, prior to the Second Vatican Council. At that time, life in the Order, and even more so for a convert brother, was very hard; going to bed at seven in the afternoon and getting up at two in the morning meant retiring to your dormitory when it was still hot and getting up when it was still hot. Moreover, they went to bed early with their woollen clothing, not just habit and scapular, but also shirt, stockings and socks. They could only take off one shoe. The brethren worked eight hours in winter and nine in summer. They lived, worked and slept without taking off their clothes. This is hardly conducive to proper hygiene, but we have to place ourselves in the shoes of the reformists: Monastic life had become relaxed due to the loose and abusive interpretations of the Rule: they reverted to the literal interpretation. Chapter 1 read: Monks sleep with their clothes on... to be ever ready." To saint Benedict, the monk is like the soldier on a campaign, and that is what he says in his Rule. That is why our dormitory led straight to the church. And when it was time to get up, everyone hastened to do so, some faster than others, to reach the church for the opus divinum, the work of God, or prayer.

Moreover, the observance of silence was so strict that no conversation whatsoever was permitted, not even at leisure time (Constitutions, no. 95). Free time was spent praying or reading, the former normally in the church. The brethren would recite the Our Father or Hail Mary in Latin. The road to sanctification lay in strict observance of the Rule."

Having thus spoke, Hermenegildo bequeaths us these brief brushstrokes on Zacarías, and a lovely reflection on silence:

"I think it is very important to establish Zacarías' perfect observance of the Rule as a solid base for his sanctity. He did his duty everywhere and at all times, silent and smiling. Whenever you met him he would always greet you with a smile.

The Trappists discovered that the smile was the best compromise between silence and charity in the relationship between brethren and guests. Some years ago, André Frossand, who died recently, wrote a book called The Salt of the Earth, *in which he describes each one of the religious Orders through their outer traits. He says that the Trappists were characterised by their smile: if you knock at the door the porter welcomes you with a smile, a smiling housekeeper shows you to your room, and any brother you meet smiles at you. And if, on going for a stroll through the garden, you encounter a monk absorbed in his reading, with his hood pulled over his head, and you feel like pulling it off to see what he does, there is no need to do so. He is smiling."*

Thank you, Hermenegildo.

And now it is the turn of Graciliano, who lived with Zacarías for over forty years. He knew him as cellarer, his trade for many years. He summarises Zacarías' life in two words: prayer and work.

Zacarías was, first and foremost, a man of prayer. In his cell, at the door, in the shop, he lived in the presence of God, and nobody could prevent this, even for the good many years that we was involved in the work on

the property with the workers and the people of Carcastillo. He was always punctual in his liturgical duties. After Morning Prayer, he would remain in prayer for a further half-hour, kneeling sort of curled up in his choir stall, and I think he even remained there a little longer. This is admirable, because at that time the convert brethren were not required to attend the choir. After the recent reform, when they freely became monks, even in the habit, they were exemplary in their punctuality when attending the choir.

His charity was exquisite. If he ever bothered a fellow brother it was only because he had to do his duty or obey the orders of his superiors. When he was the cellarer he was always in demand, and by many different people. People called him just to enjoy his conversation. But even so, nothing could perturb his intimacy with God. Events, whether or not they had to with the church, never perturbed his inner peace. He felt as if he was in God's hands. He respected the new religious ways and fashions, although he did not understand them. He once said to someone: "With all the wealth we have, what need is there for us to look for strange things?"

The good brother Florence wrote to me from Santa María de Escalonias, in Hornacheulos (Córdoba), where as an aging monk he had gone with other brothers from La Oliva to found a Cistercian House. The feat is a heroic one, akin to transplanting an old tree with deep roots. He says that his memory is poor –and is getting worse– and that he and Zacarías were never actually "on intimate terms." But he digs into his memory. And there is always something new to uncover. He thus remembers that when he entered La Oliva Zacarías was the first person to bring him a bowl of milk and bread. "He was very charitable, smiling and affectionate with everyone; and as he worked outside he had a lot of dealings with the laymen, who all loved him dearly." It was Zacarías who taught him the sign language of the monks to be able to communicate without talking, and to be a server and censer in the ceremonies. When Florencio reached La Oliva –many years ago– Zacarías was the cellarer, and was burdened with work.

> *"He had to look after fourteen workers and their horses, because at that time everything was done with horses, except threshing, which was done with a thresher, which, it must also be said, was very old. Zacarías had to assign work to the whole community besides the workers, as well as fourteen children who studied and worked there. Once he had done all his work he would go to the church, where he would spend many a long hour, always kneeling, his arms resting on the choir stall in front of him, and huddled up. At that time he was on a diet, I believe he had a stomach ulcer. He ate only rice and milk, and slept in the infirmary on an armchair as he could not sleep in a bed because of his asthma. Once I went out into the fields with him, and we said the rosary in the shelter of a steep bank. On praying the litany, he knelt down and I followed suit.*
>
> *When he fell ill he asked to be relieved of his duties, particularly his cellar tasks. But he continued to be an example to the community by dint of his simple nature, poverty and obedience, to say nothing of his kindness, as he was always affectionate with everyone, and spent a great deal of time saying rosaries. Although in the end he could not even do that. He was a good, pious and*

obedient monk, although I did not witness his death, as by then I was far away from La Oliva.

Zacarías was cellarer at the time of the Republic. They used to work with mules. The monastery's mules were the best, and therefore the envy of everyone. The brother muleteer was called Alejo, who hailed from Getafe. Zacarías was very fond of him, and a long time later chided the monks for failing to appreciate that hard worker. "After all that Alejo has done for the monastery!" he would say. "Not a word of thanks. It is as if they had failed to see what he had done."

Zacarías was plagued by the problems of irrigation, so basic for the crops: shifts and late hours, frauds... even at night. The inhabitants of Carcastillo even stole water from the monastery. One night Zacarías went out with his hoe to stand guard next to the sluice-gate, ready to give his life. As fortune would have it, nobody came by and no ill befell him.

But there are more good things to come, such as the words of Brother Vicente, former cook at the monastery. His initial answers to my questions were rather terse: "a good and simple monk", "saint-like", "pleasant and kind", "perfect", etc. To the last question, "How long did you live with Zacarías for?" he replied "ABOUT FIFTY".

Although the best part of those years must have been spent in silence, was that all brother Vicente had to tell us? I think not. When remembering his work in the "laboratory", a room annexed to the kitchen, he cooked up two simple but tasty dishes for me, which I shall talk of here. He told me things nobody else had, some of it second hand, some of it from the horse's mouth. Some of these titbits pertained to days that had long since passed, before Zacarías joined the monastery, and which were greatly illustrative of the transformation brought about in him.

He thus informs us –"I was told"– that when Zacarías was a young man he had a ferocious temper –he later uses the word brutal– and regularly thumped the young boys of the village. He even assures me that one day Zacarías challenged another boy to a duel on the mountain, although the latter did not turn up. But in the monastery he was like a daisy, the epitome of the simple and kind man. A miracle of how force can be tamed by the spirit; an utter revolution, not in the sense of the revolutionary who is bent on changing the whole world, but one in itself.

> *I met him in 1936... When I joined, he was working in the fields and was in charge of the workers there. In 1938 he was conscripted in the last drafts. He wore civilian clothes, it was the first time I had seen him dressed thus. Once he came on leave, he reverted to his habit, spent three days at the monastery and then returned to the front. I never saw him without his habit again. He didn't like to see priests and monks dressed as civilians. He loved the habit. At he end of the war he was put in charge of the orchard. He was my master cellarer in the fields. He picked up a bronchial disease and spent a few years in the infirmary, where he had to sleep in an armchair. He basically got over that, although not totally, and was then operated on for a duodenal ulcer, and was constantly ill after that. He then became a helper in the guest house, and later porter and kitchen assistant. When he stood in for me in 1979, when I went to Rome for a few*

months, he did a great job. When I returned he stayed on as my assistant for a few years, taking care of the kitchen, the door and the guest house as best he could. He was an untiring worker, and was dearly loved by all of us. He said the rosary every day in church, always kneeling. I have known few other monks, Fathers and Brethren like him."

Brother Vicente thought some more about Zacarías in his free time, and has recalled more impressions which he now shares with us:

"While I never actually heard him talk about his experience of God, the latter was evidently present in his work, carried out in a spirit of faith and in silent prayer which, as Brother Rafael María would say "the thoughts of God flow through the silent soul, and not through the soul of the dissolute and talkative monk". "He was exemplary, punctual and constant in community life. As soon as the bells rang out he would immediately stop what he was doing, and follow the orders of Saint Benedict. He was charitable with the community and outsiders alike, as he had dealings with the latter in his tasks as cellarer and later in the guest house and the door. It is good to meet laymen who speak well of a brother, as many did in the case of Zacarías.

Zacarías' main and favourite reading matter were the lives of the Saints, and particularly the Bible. I Sometimes saw him read and reread the prologue to the Gospel of Saint John. I remember some of the advice he gave me: "Do not run, take your time and do things in the love of God. God never hurries." He also said to me: "Imitate Jesus, not men. Many of your colleagues will seem to be saints, but take a closer look and you will see that the seven capital sins are bubbling inside them. And thus the saying comes true: The novice seems like a saint but is not. The middle-aged monk neither seems nor is one. The elderly monk does not seem so but is, because God has purified him though great adversity, which is why he is silent".

In his last disease, I personally witnessed...

Brother Vicente, let us follow Zacarías' advice: Do not run, wait until Zacarías' last illness arrives and then we shall come back to you.

But fifty years together is a long time. Perhaps Brother Vicente is like the farm-worker from Álava who went to confession once a year and began by saying to his confessor "Wring the truth out of me." I returned to La Oliva precisely to "wring" some more out of Brother Vicente, a cook for fifty years. When he went to Rome for a month he stayed for six, and it was Zacarías who stood in for him, and who actually wrote to him telling him of his difficulties and scolding him for delaying his return. "I wrote back to him and said: Do not despair and stay the course, because nobody ever remembers a coward". Vicente knew Onofre, the priest who had referred Zacarías to La Oliva, and his sister Vicenta, who once said of her brother: "This man will leave me with nothing, he is always helping the poor... And she was right. One day she went to Roncesvalles and died there.

"Vicente, you told me that Zacarías had fought in the Civil War, in 1936."

"And he did. He was called up in the last draft in 1938. When he took up arms he shaved his beard off. He looked like a young boy. He served in Aragon. One night he was on

guard and he encountered someone from Carcastillo who was on the other side. They recognised each other, because Zacarías was well known. I don't know how, but he got the other man's papers sorted out and sent him home. I met him in the village."

"And what did he do when he was the cellarer?"

"He worked hard and made others work hard as well. When the irrigation was started up there were a lot of problems with the villagers. They used to steal the water at night. I remember one man stabbed another and Zacarías promptly loaded the wounded man onto his cart, took him back to the monastery and healed him."

"But wasn't he always ill?"

"Yes, at the beginning and for years after he had asthma, and he had to sleep sitting up in the infirmary. I think he actually went to see a faith healer in Pamplona who applied some pitch patches to his chest and his back. Then he had his stomach thing, and lived on milk and rice. He was taken to Hospital. Quite a change, because in the past hardly anyone ever left the convent. They did everything there, sewed you up and that was that. After his operation his gut opened, the stitches I mean, and they fixed that. I think that that was when he met some Arabs in the hospital. He loved them deeply, perhaps because he had done his military service in Africa. When he was taken to hospital, Brother Rafael told him he had cancer and that he was going to die. He was admitted again, years later, on December 26, 1984, and went with Father Carbonell, but they brought him back to the monastery to die. Do you know something? Once, I don't know why, Zacarías said to Father Luis Bermejo: "I don't want to be beatified. What for? For another feast day… which will be profaned anyway."

He also talked to me about Alejo, the muleteer: "*He came to the monastery when he was 16, with the boys who were around at the time. Then he left, got married and settled down in Carcastillo, but he visited the monastery a lot.*" "And when his wife died" –as Abbot Francisco tells me– "He came back to live in the monastery, and there he died, and was buried with cowl and ceremony, just like any monk."

So you can see how much I was eventually able to "wring" out of Brother Vicente. And then some more.

And following tradition, we shall close the procession of witnesses with Father Mariano, Abbot of the monastery towards the end of Zacarías' life. I had a long interview with him in Lecumberri, where he taught the nuns Exercises. He was a great admirer of Zacarías, whose spirit he knew like no one else. When the position of Abbot became vacant in 1969, the Order sent a Visitor to carry out a kind of survey as to the possible substitute. Mariano enjoyed the greatest support among the monks. He had taken his orders but one month before, and therefore did not have the canonical age to hold the position. He asked for some time to think about it before the Tabernacle. On leaving the Visitor's room he ran into Zacarías, who was a great, albeit unqualified, psychologist, and who asked him what was wrong. Mariano opened his soul to him. "Go to the Tabernacle, but you must accept anyway." "I spent one hour alone with Jesus, who did not speak to me, but when I went back to the Visitor's room, I said to him: Jesus has given me no guidance, but Brother Zacarías told me to accept it."

And that is how became the first Superior of the community (1969-1972) and then Abbot (1972-1993).

The Abbot Mariano has a lot of tasty things to say of Zacarías.

"In his later years Zacarías had more contact with the outside, and people loved him dearly. Do you know that he was a great matchmaker? He didn't like people to be single, he wanted to see them married. And his matchmaking brought a good many couples together. Some people have some very funny stories to tell: "I know who I wanted to marry", "I made myself available". There are so many people that remember him!

He was a great counsellor. When they wanted to appoint me Abbot, I was reluctant, but I talked to Zacarías and it was he who made me take the decision. I used to ask him for advice on many things. He was special. He was always in the right place at the right time, and what is more he always said the right thing. You hardly noticed his presence, because he was always there. He never asked me for anything, and never complained about anything either. Sometimes I think I did not take good enough care of him, maybe he needed something, a habit, a new vest, shoes, I don't know... Zacarías was rather special.

He was a transparent soul, the name of Jesus was always on his lips, and he spoke his name with warmth, with delight, because for him it was the solution to everything. He was just different, the best-loved, a well-known saint in Ribera de Navarra. Mysticism was born in him, it was so natural in him. He died like a saint. I don't now how, but I am sure that we shall see Zacarías on the altar."

A lovely flower to give the bouquet its finishing touch.

VI
LIKE A WHISPER

There is a secret in the life of Zacarías, which is difficult to hide, although it is almost unfathomable. There is one anecdote that gives us an insight into it. Some time in the forties Zacarías received a visit from Mr. Ferrin Lezaun, the parish priest of Yerri, the village where Zacarías' grandparents were from and where he had relatives. Fermín, a great admirer of the holiness of the simple bother, reached the monastery's orchard. A monk was working away with his hoe and was cleaning the furrows of vegetables. It was him! It must have been about eleven o'clock on a blazing hot summer morning. "Zacarías!" said the good priest. He turned round, smiling, holding the hoe in his left hand. Fermín gently chided him: "Zacarías, what are you doing working at this time, and in such heat?!" Zacarías, with his ineffable smile, pointed towards the apse of the monastery with his index finger, and simply replied:

"For him, for him. For Jesus."

And his smile grew even wider.

The mystery of the monk is intriguing to the mundane. They fail to understand it. How could they ever understand an answer like the one we have just heard? But nevertheless, that answer, apparently elemental, simple, holds the key to everything. The convert brother does not come to the monastery just to work, to be a beast of burden for the community, but to search for God, Jesus, God made flesh, nearby, through silence, prayer… and work. **For Jesus**. Shall we call that a private confession?, and Zacarías "convict and converted?" Could there be a better observation, a better experience, of a rule that is invoked in the Uses?

> It is of the utmost importance not to forget that work is not only a punishment, but also a powerful medium of sanctification for he who applies himself to supernaturalise it. The brethren –says the Venerable Reformer of the Trappists– will take to their work with affection, energy and humility. They will occupy their spirits with high thoughts which the very nature of their work will suggest to them in abundance. In this way they will become veritable imitators of the ancient solitaries, whose life was one of prolonged prayer, since when their hands were constantly occupied with work, their spirit was constantly elevated towards heaven."

Take to their work with *affection, energy and humility*. As the hands become callused and the body sweats, the spirit is in Heaven, or what is the same, next to the tabernacle concealed in the church apse. For him, for Jesus!

This scene, but one little flower in the life of Zacarías, reminds me of a similar utterance of Saint Paul, very simple in appearance, but of great depth. Mihi vivere Christus est (Phil. 1.21). For me to live is Christ. To understand such an utterance one must evoke ways of life based solely on one element or value, be it good or bad, which dominates everything. Some people live almost exclusively for money, pleasure, sex, sport, art... They live –and dream– of money, social status, gastronomic whims, success, power. The professional tennis player or swimmer dedicates some seven or eight hours daily to their favourite sport, like the musician to the violin or piano. They live for and on... their greatest and truest treasure, their dominant, almost exclusive value. This is their gospel (Mathew 6,21). *Your treasure lies where your heart is*. If we invert this maxim we have a good compass that will help us to trace the true delights and orientation of the human heart: where your heart really lies, then so too will your greatest treasure be found, what you really regard as a treasure.

The centre which, like a magnet, attracted and focused the life of Zacarías every day, over the years, is summarised in this name, Jesus, the name "that is sweet to recall", as the Cistercian monk Saint Bernard would say.

Before joining, Manuel frequented the monastery in an attempt to be sure of his vocation, and met Zacarías in the doorway. "Pray for me, brother, so that God may help me and that I may come soon to the monastery", he would say to Zacarías on departing. And Zacarías would reply "Yes, I shall pray for you. But if you come, may it be for Jesus and Jesus alone." Later, when he was in the monastery as a guest, he realised that Zacarías spoke little to the guests and always laced his conversations with expressions such as "You, love Jesus as best you can", "Everything we do is for Jesus", "Jesus will help us to do everything". But, as the same witness tells us, what most impressed people was "the way he said it, with his habitual smile and penetrating gaze, full of tenderness."

At the end of his life, when he was in the Hospital, on saying goodbye to the friends and relatives that went to visit him, he would say: "We have seen each other. Now leave me alone with Jesus for a while." And as the monk who was with him would sometimes suggest that certain visits were rather long and arduous, he would reply: "We must thank them for their good intentions, the problem is that they do not let us lead our life."

Another witness, who as a novice used to visit him in the infirmary, heard him say: "You, love Jesus with all your might. How Jesus loves us! We must fall in love with Jesus!" And he emphasised *the way* he said these words: "He said these sentences with the utmost conviction and belief, drawing out the name of Jesus, which sort of lingered on and echoed out, as if knocking on the door of one's heart."

Jesus, a name anchored in his heart, the centre of his life and all his love, his reason for living, the steady horizon of his death. The name sprang from the depth of his spirit, not as an ostentatious proclamation or a rousing speech, but like a simple whisper... but oh so true! Did William Johnston not write that the only art of Christian prayer is being in love with God, who is love, of allowing ourselves to be "lovingly hypnotised by Jesus"? And Zacarías' heart sailed through these shining realms.

The prophet Elias, when threatened with death by Jezebel, and having taken refuge on Mount Horeb, heard a voice which said to him: "The Lord will come by. Stand up... A hurricane ensued, which tore up the mountain and smashed the rocks, but the Lord was not in the wind. The wind was followed by an earthquake, but the Lord was not in the earthquake. After the earthquake came fire, but the Lord was not in the fire. Then, a gentle breeze was heard. Elias covered his face with his cloak. The Lord was in the gentle breeze (1 Kings 19, 11-2).

Zacarías' life has no great deeds. He did not write erudite treatises on Christology, and neither did he give any fire and brimstone sermons from pulpits or in public squares. But the name of Jesus… barely whispered by Zacarías… "that gentle breeze" –embodied the Lord. Either when he would say it to himself, for the solace of this soul, or when he whispered it to the ears of others, or better still, to the heart of others…

I was told that one day a young female journalist went to visit La Oliva intending to write a pointed article on monastic life. When she was least expecting it, she met Zacarías in the doorway, who blurted out at her:

"Do you know him?"

"Know… who?", responded the puzzled journalist.

"Jesssusss", whispered Zacarías.

It came like a sudden blow, as if she had been jolted by an unexpected electric shock. The young girl moved off, deeply perturbed, and entered the solitary temple, unable to forget that word, that face, that gaze. And she sat down a while. When she decided to leave the monastery, she met Zacarías once again at the door, who looked at her squarely and said:

"He touched you, didn't he? Do not leave him, do not leave him."

The name of Jesus, *dulce melos*, sweet melody for the ears, whose utterance led Zacarías' spirit to become one with a supernatural, founding, all-embracing and all-involving world, and which at the same time he longed for more and more as the definitive endpoint of his life. Growing plenitude and thirst at the same time. On one occasion his soul bared the following utterance, which, if we look into it further, produces vertigo: "What do the saints in Heaven have that I do not! I have Jesus!"

And with Jesus, Mary. It could hardly be otherwise in a Bernard monk, which is how the Cistercians were known in Spain. One monk tells me that Mary was his other "weakness". What do we mean when we attribute such a "weakness" to someone? A child who is over-fond of a granny or an aunt, liking things spick and span at all times, fussing over a meal we are making, adoring music, being enthusiastic about something or someone... is a weakness. Everything else falls apart, collapses or sinks, before such a weakness. The point of the weakness is something long and deeply rooted in a person, it is stable, steady, it cannot be foregone, it is loved above everything else. Jesus was Zacarías' "weakness"; the other, closely related, was Mary. One monk told me that his admiration for the Mother of God was immense, and that he was proud to bear her name in his surname, Santamaría (literally Holy Mary). "Mary, fall in love with Mary, Ventura", he said to another monk, who tells me: "I have no idea how many rosaries Zacarías must have prayed in his life. While he was not working, his rosary beads were in his hands at all times, caressing them everywhere, at all times, as he went about praying the Hail Mary."

One day, another colleague and great admirer, who sometimes worked with him in the kitchen, decided to try to trick him playfully, to see how he reacted:

"Zacarías, shall we talk about politics?"

"What! Talk politics!?" he responded, his brow creased, rather disconcerted.

It was as if someone had proposed talking about advanced mathematics. But the playful trickster immediately began to say the rosary, with the ritual "Lord, open my lips..." Zacarías smiled, he had got the joke and delightfully followed suite. Subsequently, on meeting the would-be joker in the kitchen, it was Zacarías who took up the joke and suggested:

"José, let's talk politics."

Saying the Rosary does not require a lot of thinking. You simply let yourself be carried lovingly by the words of the Angel Gabriel to Mary, a reminder of that transcendental moment in her life, and a crucial point from the creation of the world to the end for believers. The Rosary... The Bible of the poor, much more than the stained glass window of the cathedrals, which only the experts understand.

How many Rosaries would Zacarías have said, and how would he have said them? It was his regular prayer. Ingrained in his subconscious, and even in his conscience, was the memory of his father, Tirso, who said the daily Rosary in the kitchen in Oteiza. "Let us say the Rosary the way father used to in the kitchen", he said to his younger brother José, who had gone to visit him in the monastery. That implicit gesture spliced his monastery life and his family roots, as old and far-off memories still lingered inside him. Prayer bound and united everything, fusing past, present and future in an atmosphere of tranquil and steadfast eternity. He would often say the Rosary in church before Vespers. And he would also say it whenever he had some free time.

Towards the end of his days, when he could no longer make it down to the kitchen even to peel potatoes, he would spend his time saying rosaries. All the beads he used and prayed with bore the essence of his own personal form of prayer. Every rosary was like the first one. He told someone that the seeds he used to make his rosaries –popularly known as the "pips of the Virgin"– had been made by God so that they could make rosaries with them.

Some readers might wonder what Zacarías used to nurture his spirit. Or more specifically, where his inspiration came from, what he read. The so-called *lectio divina* is a sacred practice in monastic life. It may have been neglected somewhat at the beginning of the restoration of La Oliva, but it later became regular practice. Reading is the human watering trough which enriches the spirit. Zacarías always practiced it in the monks' so-called common office, where each one could keep their favourite books, and those reserved for their use. The Kempis was one of his favourites. It had also been a favourite of Saint Theresa, who called it "the partridge" of spiritual books; of Saint Ignatius of Loyola and so many others. And in our time of Bonhoefer himself.

Someone hinted that he preferred Spanish mystics, Saint Theresa and Saint John of the Cross. Another monk was more explicit, and told me the following anecdote: "I remember I was reading Saint Theresa behind the greenhouse. Zacarías usually walked round that way in mid-afternoon, because the ground was paved there. It was still sunny. We approached each other and exchanged a smile, in silence. But on the day in question he walked up to me and asked: "What are you reading?" On showing him the book, he replied, his face beaming with satisfaction: *"It is all in there, everything is in there. Never leave it, because everything is in there."*

She is the new Doctor of the Universal Church, to the outrage of some, who shares the title with sagacious men such as Saint Thomas Aquinus, Saint Buenaventura, Saint Robert Belarmine, etc. She discovered the humble little path of trust and love, she wished to be the heart of the Church: "I understood –she says in *Exclamations of the Soul to God*– that only love leads members of the church to act, and that if there were no love the apostles would not have written the gospel or the blood of the martyrs would not have been shed. I clearly recognised, and am convinced, that love is present in all vocations, that love is all, that it spans all times and places, and that in a word love is eternal."

What mysterious harmony took place between her spirituality and that of Zacarías, both of them kneaded in love?

However, there is one that stands out over all others, from the Holy Scriptures, and within it the Gospel of

Saint John, the great lover and messenger of love. "God is Love" (Jo 4,8) "Nobody has greater love than he who Gives life" (Jo 15, 13), "he loved them to the extreme" (Jo 13, 1), "Love one another" (Jo 3,23): There are so many ways into the unfathomable mystery. We have already learnt that he read and reread the fourth gospel, that awe-inspiring page where all history is condensed and is set within eternity. *In principio erat Verbum*. How would this echo in Zacarías' soul. We shall never know.

I seem to discover a minimum spark of John in an anecdote the new Abbot told me. He recalled how on one occasion the monks of La Oliva went on an excursion to the monastery of Liere, which centuries before had been populated by Cistercians. The Abbot sat down on the bus next to Zacarías. They made the journey in silence. All of a sudden Zacarías uttered a phrase, as if engrossed and unaware of what was going on around him: "A little fish... made with love!" The Abbot did not know how to interpret the case.

"Wouldn't it have been in Easter week?" I said. "That is when the appearance of Jesus by the lakeside is read, where he waited for the apostles with a fish on embers (Jo 21,9). Perhaps Zacarías was absorbed in meditation on that passage from the gospel, and he uttered, without realising that he had heard him, that mysterious phrase, emphasising the delicacy and the love of Jesus? Might his humble kitchen work, carried out with love, not have contributed to such illumination?

We trace fire through smoke. Through readings, typical expressions, we seek to track the innermost nooks and crannies of the spirit of Zacarías. Where the name of Jesus, as whispered by him, bubbles over inside, as if only it were valid, solid, absolutely absolute.

Jesus, Mary, John the Baptist... the waters that propel the mill. But the mill is the spirit of Zacarías, either at work or at prayer. We know that he thought of Jesus while digging with his hoe. I know not whether hard work with mules and farm workers is conducive to lofty meditation. It was well known –and in Navarra they believed this was borne out by experience– that mules would only bear their load when yelled upon to do, yells that distracted grammarians would define as mere interjections and moralists as the slackest blasphemies. Is it not said that a mayor strictly prohibited the uttering of blasphemies, even to coax obstinate mules, unless "it was to get them up the hill?"

Such was the specific environment of the first Zacarías, before withdrawing to the kitchen or the door.

It is true that Saint Bernard, when talking about the work of the monks, circa the 12th Century, had found a strange shortcut to wisdom: "Follow my advice, based on my experience, trustingly" he says in letter 109. "And do not forget that you will learn more in the forest than from books; wood and stones will teach you more than the wise masters." The truth is that La Oliva does not abound in lush forests. However, the cold North Wind in winter, the special light of spring with the birth of the sowing season and the trees in blossom once again, the annual arrival of the storks to the heights of the monastery, the so-often uncertain summer harvest, the warm South wind in autumn, when the leaves fall and the grapes are harvested would surely speak to Zacarías' soul in their perennially different language. Nobody has talked to me about his oneness with the land, its changing nature, the yearly miracle of the harvest that meant so much to the subsistence of the monastery.

It is agreed that the "divine office" means, in monastic uses, prayer at liturgical times, the crowning moment of worship. But is not working with the sweat of one's brow also a divine office, as it was imposed by God (Gen. 3,19)?

Zacarías faithfully observed both. "A hundred percent worker" as someone said. In the hours set for working, naturally. Because at other times, and even when working –Zacarías was a "one hundred per cent "prayer"". "I am always at prayer" he wrote to someone. For him praying was as natural as breathing. Not an act, but a permanent state. That is why he was so fond of Sundays, the day he loved best, when he had more time to further his spirit. While poor people hurry and hasten, urgent to fill their so-called leisure time, free time on Sundays afforded Zacarías a tranquil and joyous respite for his business –as opposed to leisure–: being alone with Jesus on Sunday, the "day of the Lord."

> *"Zacarías himself told me this"* recalls his brother José. *"For me all days are holy, devoted to love and to serve God in prayer and in work. But Sunday afternoons are even holier. Between 2 and 6 in the afternoon our time is our own: rest, read, stroll... So I go to the church, and I settle down in my spot in the choir stall. And there,*

happy, tranquil and content, I spend the afternoon hours with Jesus."

Have you realised how many mention that when he prayed he was mostly kneeling? Modern man has lost the sense of adoration, of humble surrender to that which so infinitely overwhelms us, and even dares to proclaim to the four winds "The God in whom I believe" or the God in whom I do not believe", as if God had to suit him, his poor mind, and if he could be a measure of God. The Moslems are much more deeply religious, as it would never cross their mind to ask God questions, let alone argue with him.

Besides kneeling, And this is also underlined by many, Zacarías prayed with his head between his hands, curled up, like a ball of wool, his body bent, and his soul, as if to visibly receive or unravel in his bosom some mystery. Someone, who was both moved and intrigued by the silent figure of the praying Zacarías, spoke at length on the question with him one day:

"Zacarías, when you are in the church praying like a statue, what are you thinking, what do you say? Sometimes I can't think of anything and I am curious about it. I would like to kneel down next to you and have you say your thoughts or feelings out loud so that I could know."

And Zacarías answered, almost with a fable worthy of the Fathers of the Desert: "Have you ever seen a pair of sweethearts that go out walking on a cold and rainy day and take shelter in a doorway? They say nothing to each other, they are freezing cold but they are happy... because they are together. Well so am I. I say nothing, because I am happy in the company of the Lord."

"I say nothing." Silence, rather than inner or outer words. It is metaphysical. Nothing... before he who is All. The summit of mystical experience. Is it that there are fewer mysteries than we imagine in Zacarías' soul, or perhaps a mystery so deep that we cannot even begin to imagine it?

VII
IN THE AUTUMN OF LIFE

The phrase is well known, it is by Saint John of the Cross: "When evening comes you will be examined in love" (Sayings, 59). Yes, the evening of life, the melancholic evening, twilight, on the threshold of death, our twilight of life on earth. One monk told me that Zacarías was one of the few people whom he heard in La Oliva say that he was not afraid to die, *at that very moment*.

Dying is one thing, having to abandon the monastery to die is a different matter altogether, particularly to someone like Zacarías. In fact, the last time he had to leave it was not the first. Around 1964 he had been operated on for a massive stomach ulcer. He had half his stomach removed. The doctor was amazed that he was still alive. He was told that he had cancer, although it turned out that someone had got the x-rays mixed up and that it was someone else. Around 1975 and in later years he spent three winters in Hospital for a lung complaint. He spent a few months in the tuberculosis unit. He had a really bad time at the hands of some dreadful male nurses who pulled his leg, but he eventually changed them all.

This time was his last visit to the Hospital of Pamplona. He was accompanied by Brother Vicente. His cancer had spread and the doctors gave him a fortnight to live. On the way, the Brother told him that was going to die, to which Zacarías replied: "That is fine, as very soon I shall be with Jesus!" When they reached the Hospital the nurses told the brother not to tell Zacarías the nature of his condition under any circumstances. "But I told him on the way here and he is happy to die!" The nurses couldn't believe it. After a long spate of tests in hospital the doctor came to his room and said: "We made a mistake, it isn't cancer, you are just weak." Zacarías' first words were: "Well you really put your foot in it!... Here was I happy to be going to meet Jesus! And now I'm going to have to stay here!" The doctors and the nurses couldn't believe their ears.

Pilar and Julia are a never-ending source of anecdotes. They had both worked at chambermaids at the Hotel Maisonave in Pamponam and are friends. Pilar was always with Zacarías in hospital, even when the monk was not there. She used to send ice-creams to the monastery on Zacarías' birthday –June 10– and has continued to do so since his death. And Julia Alfaro –does the surname ring a bell?– yes, she was a daughter of the family that fostered Zacarías when his father passed away. Memories well up in their heads, and they hardly let each other get a word in edgeways.

They told me that Zacarías had a very uncouth roommate, who swore and blasphemed all the time, and did not want to share the room with a monk. Zacarías eventually tamed and transformed him and he died like a saint. His family attended Zacarías' funeral. One day the nurse put him through a veritable ordeal when trying to find his vein. Someone mentioned the butchery later, but Zacarías simply responded: "My God, I felt sorry for the poor nurse!" On another occasion a rather sloppy male nurse bathed him in cold water, and those who were with Zacarías evidently brought the question up, but Zacarías replied: "The poor man didn't even realise. And we are good friends now." Even so, his first bath with hot water and bubble bath must have been heavenly, and totally new to him, as he mentioned excitedly: "Some really nice girls gave me a bath!" Zacarías was a bag of skin and bones, and the nurses joked with him as they bathed him. "You are a real beauty!" cracked one of them, although her colleague, somewhat more realistic, quipped: "Put the plug in the bath or he might slip though the hole."

The good monk won over everyone over at the Hospital. Some student of Christianity took a group to see him, probably because he wanted to show them a saint in the flesh, a man of God. One of them stayed to keep him company a little longer, with a very telling explanation: "Excuse me, ma'am, but I don't want to go, it isn't every day that one sees a saint."

There are some very intimate confidences from those days. "I haven't committed a sin for thirty years." And even more stunning: "I do not know if heaven will be better." He was brimming over, saturated with joy.

"How can you say that when your body is covered with sores?" said someone.

"Yes, but the greater the suffering the greater the pleasure." God has given me a dessert: Pleasure: I can hardly imagine what heaven will be like..."

When the course of his disease was already irreversible and the end was nigh, Zacarías was given the greatest gift he could have received at the time: he was to return to La Oliva to die. Surprisingly, his unwavering joy seem to falter. He went through a supreme test, which a monk explained to me:

About a fortnight before his death his spirit was put severely to the test, plunged into total darkness. He could see nothing. The conversation always revolved around the same subject, how happy he had been in La Oliva. "But now I see NOTHING, NOTHING, NOTHING." His face did not show any anguish, but lost its smile. I visited him every day to understand what he was going through. The greeting was always the same, as was his reply:

"Zacarías, is the darkness still upon you?

"Yes, Ventura. For years He has been giving things to me. Now it is my turn."

One or two days before he died, he said to me:

"It's all over. I am happier than ever."

I new that he was getting ready for that journey. On Saint Bernard's day, when I was in the dairy, Brother Rafael came to break the news. I knew that Zacarías had passed away before he opened his mouth.

The truth is that Zacarías had dreamt of making that last journey on the Assumption. He who had loved the Virgin. As the day went by and that supreme moment had still not arrived, he expressed his new desire: "The Virgin does not want to take me. It will be Saint Bernard's day." In the evening, at nightfall, he received the viaticum… and he went to say one more Rosary to the lady of his heart. It was still like one greets one's lover: "Hail Mary… Holy Mary, Mother of God." Only this time the parts which read "pray for us…" and "now and at the hour of our death" were no longer necessary. Zacarías' question, What will heaven be like?, had been answered.

News of his death spread. People came from all around, Carcastillo, Mélida, Murillo el Fruto, who all adored him, crammed into the naves of the temple to look upon his face for the last time –Oh! Without that smile that nobody would forget! And then they saw him fly off in the form of that strange little bird. Even the most diehard enemies of messages of the spirit must have thought, deep down inside: I don't know if heaven exists, but if it does then Zacarías must be there: that much is clear, much clearer than this immaculately blue August sky.

Not long ago, the community celebrated All Souls' Day in the monastery cemetery. A portable altar is placed in the centre amid the trees for Holy Mass to be said. It is a plastic way of experiencing the mystery of the communion of the Saints, all together: those who are still in the world, and those who have passed on to the other life. Some of the monks, rather out of the way, did not see what happened. Others did, and they assure me that it was true. During the ceremony there were two butterflies that flew constantly from Zacarías' tomb to the altar and then back to the tomb, flying over other tombs on their way. What was the meaning of the butterflies' preference for Zacarías' tomb, Zacarías' attraction and message for the altar, where his Jesus was concealed? Could it be a distinction from heaven towards his tomb, and a premonition that Zacarías is on his way… to the altar?

Table of contents

PHOTOGRAPHS